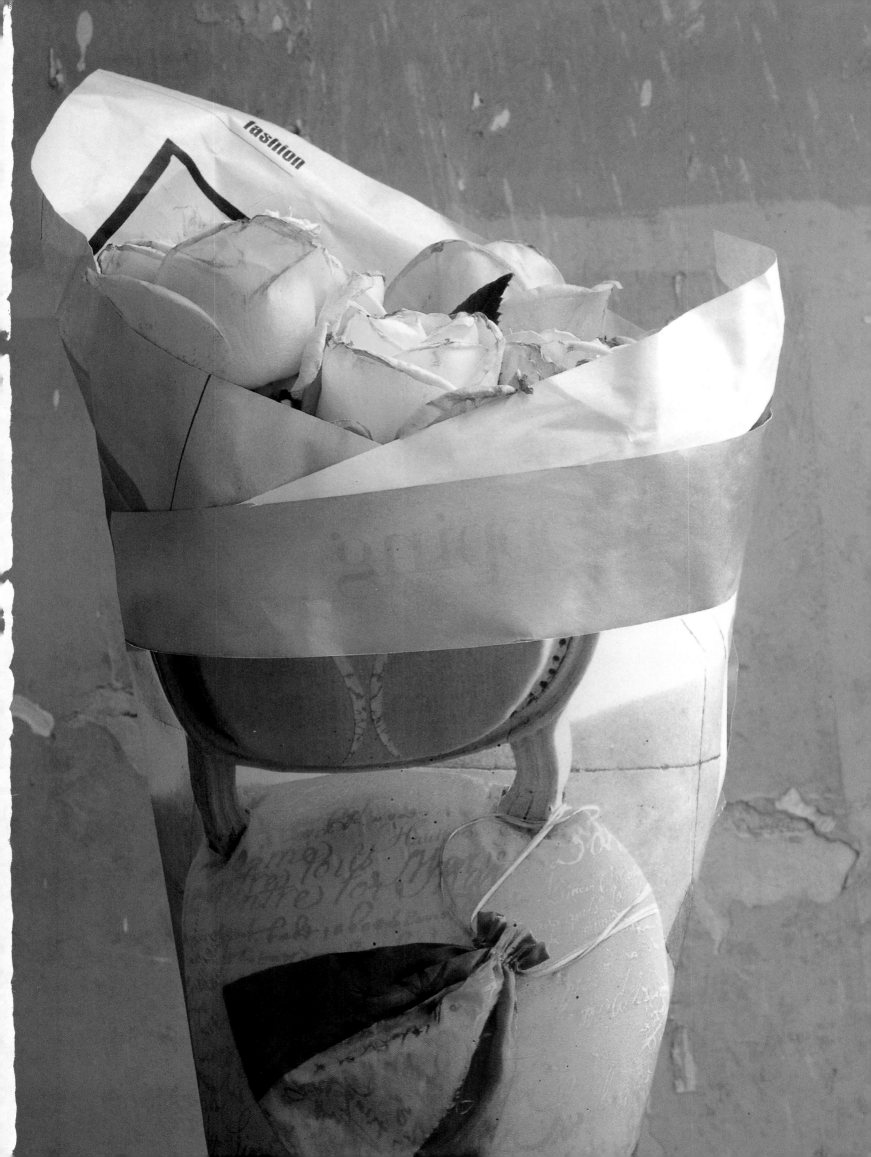

Carolyn Quartermaine
UNWRAPPED

Special Photography by Jacques Dirand
Text by Kate Constable

conran
OCTOPUS

TO MY PARENTS,
FOR THEIR LOVE AND VERVE

First published in 1997 by
Conran Octopus Limited
37 Shelton Street
London WC2H 9HN

British Library Cataloguing-in-Publication Data
A catalogue record for this book is available from the British Library
ISBN 1 85029 853 X

Commissioning Editor: Denny Hemming
Senior Editor: Catriona Woodburn
Editorial Assistant: Paula Hardy

Art Director: Helen Lewis
Designer: Peter Butler

Picture Researcher: Claire Limpus
Production Controller: Julia Golding

Produced by Mandarin
Printed in China

Contents

Introduction

By DONNA KARAN

We all know that paths can cross in very strange ways, stirring energy in both a real-life way and in an artistic way, reaching from both sides of the Atlantic and across the continents.

Like every designer, I pull pages from magazines for inspiration and color from other walks of life besides fashion, and we each in our own way find something stimulating and directional in these images. Returning to New York from London a while ago, I took with me some beautiful pages that spoke to me so much that I carried one picture around with me for over a year.

Back in London many months later, I was taken to meet an artist whom a friend said I must see. As I walked into the room I realized I had walked into the picture I had been carrying around. My first words were 'Where is your gold cement bathtub?' The artist stared at me in utter amazement. I never saw the bathtub, but I found an artist who understood color, fabric and quality with a true sensitivity. It was my first meeting with Carolyn Quartermaine.

From the first moment, a relationship began — it was a great experience to see art and fashion coming together in fabrics, articulating the body in color, form and shape. We recognized our similar sensibilities — with an emphasis on art, inspired by antiquities, an understanding of the detailing and the patina — and I recognized Carolyn's individual touch and nuance.

Now I don't have to look through magazines for Carolyn's work — those tear sheets are highlighted and collected, inspiring at all times, in one place — this wonderful book. Enjoy!

LONDON

The Total Look

'You have to be totally immersed in your own world, making it stronger and stronger. You can't dilute that world, or you lose its spirit and it becomes untrue.' Carolyn Quartermaine is sitting at her silver-topped worktable, dressed in a simple t-shirt and with a length of her own silk wrapped around her body into a skirt. The French windows to her flower-laden balcony have been thrown open to let in the scent of lavender and the birdsong from the garden square beyond.

It is one of those beautiful, sunny mornings in London and she is drinking good coffee (a half-and-half blend of Colombian and mocha beans) from a thick, white, Swedish cup. 'The basis of all that I do is art,' she acknowledges. 'My home is my studio, and my rooms reveal my ideas in process. Changes come about because *I* am changing and growing in my work. Life isn't at a standstill; neither is my house.'

Collage — the assembling of a mixture of elements — is fundamental to Carolyn Quartermaine's vision, both for its own sake and as a catalyst for fresh, artistic departures.

*'In art, there are no barriers. Colour is about texture,
is about shape ... everything leads into everything else.'*

*A slightly surreal arrange-
ment of beautiful objects is
part of the Quartermaine
style. A silk-upholstered
and collaged chair plays
glamorous tea table for a
rose-filled pastry cone; a
packet of Japanese sweets
stands in for a vase.
Overleaf: the pared-down
simplicity, freshness and
delicacy of this classic
Swedish interior provides
inspiration for artist
Carolyn Quartermaine.*

Despite her protestations that her apartment is unfinished, the room she is sitting in — the sum of her current work — seems perfect. There are walls the colour of swan's down, a gilded salon chair covered in a sublime 1960s blue-and-white print, and a bed half-submerged in a drift of snowy white linen. There are curtains the colour of pink, sugared almonds and as full-skirted as a debutante's ball gown, and on a pretty dish, pale pink, silk-covered cardboard hearts have been piled up like profiteroles. Everywhere there are lengths of her delicious textiles: printed and painted silks in every colour imaginable (and previously unimaginable) thrown over chairs, peeping out from boxes, or cut up into squares that will later be pieced together into cushions.

It's a look of pure romance. And although Carolyn Quartermaine seems to have plundered the past for her inspiration, with lines of old-fashioned italic script dancing across the seat of a French Empire-style chair, her work, with its surprising colours and technical virtuosity, is very much about the present. But then she is a thoroughly modern artist who, since studying fine art at Cheltenham and leaving London's Royal College of Art with an MA in textile design, has refused to be limited by preconceived ideas of how an artist should work. She started by creating collages, hand-painted fabrics and ceramics, and to these talents has since added furniture and rug design, styling, art direction and teaching. There are no barriers between her life and her art. Everything she does, whether it's chopping into a 1960s print dress to make a trimming for a drawstring bag, or driving halfway across Europe with a vanload of furniture to find the perfect backdrop for a photographic shoot, is evidence of her style.

Of course it takes her 'eye' — her own special way of seeing — to put together a look that is romantic and at the same time modern. Seeing the beauty in a finely carved and gilded sofa is one thing, affording the same prominence to a rusted metal garden chair or a pile of paper-bound books is another. But what characterizes Quartermaine's style is her ability to see beauty in the most unlikely objects and then to mix them with elegant eclecticism in the most delightful way.

Carolyn Quartermaine's look has evolved straight out of her work as an artist; she produces exquisite collages of fabrics, all of which she has dyed and printed, gilded and distressed until they look like beautiful scraps salvaged from a collection of ancient ball gowns. She uses papers too, printing them in italic script or covering them in hand-drawn gilded scrolls until they too look old and beautiful, like pages torn from a private notebook.

But it is the playing with and placing of these materials that is the real art — with results that are spontaneous and fresh. For as in art, so in life. When Quartermaine decorates a room, it is as if her sketchbook has come to life: everywhere objects are placed as if they are about to be drawn. Different pieces are pulled together by an inspired use of colour, shape or texture. Cushions made from broad strips of brightly coloured silk sewn together, are piled against the softly rubbed gilding of a metal chair; a piece of Indian embroidered cloth is used to cover a 1960s space-age stool; while on bookshelves, delicate flower-patterned plates

A dream-like world is in part achieved by the use of reflective surfaces. The combination of gold and silver, offset by white, adds to the aura of beautiful otherness. Silver in these schemes is suggestive of frosting. Silvered dragées look as if they have been cut from the embroidery on an Art Nouveau gown. Gold drops are metamorphosed into three-dimensional versions of the fabric design on which they sit. The hazy silvering of old mirror glass reflects slender scrolls flowing in gold and white from champagne bottles. The purity of the setting and the formality of the furniture placement are sharpened in contrast with the heavily embroidered cloth, creating an atmosphere brooding with silent, suspended anticipation.

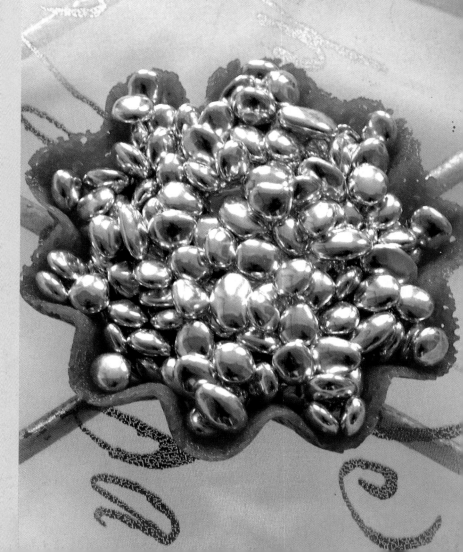

stand in for well-thumbed paperbacks. These are all elements which, although they might at first appear disparate, are brought together with an assured confidence, so that each surface — each page from that three-dimensional sketchbook — becomes a coherent aesthetic statement. She puts her stamp on everything around her. Even on chairs that have nothing piled on them you will notice that the silk has been randomly printed and then hand-painted with full-blown roses. With the gold of the chair back framing the fabric, it could be imagined that a painting had been propped there, waiting to be hung.

Quartermaine's home is an artistic laboratory where she handpaints lengths of silk and designs furniture. 'I have always been drawn to artists and their studios,' she says. 'There is something about those spaces that is so charged, so exciting. . . . With all those materials and tools spread around, it's as if you are getting a glimpse of someone's innermost thoughts.' If that is the case, then Quartermaine's thoughts are finely detailed and exquisitely coloured — reveries of a world where a tea plate balanced precariously on a chair seems like the perfect place for a pastry cone spilling

roses, damp and dewy from the garden; where lavender-grey books are placed in a glass cabinet, each book with a single pink shell positioned precisely on its cover.

You can't escape the fairy-tale quality of the fabrics, furniture and interiors that Quartermaine creates. And while everything she touches is not quite turned to gold, it is dipped, dyed, embroidered and gilded until it has gloss and lustre. 'I have a love of gold and pale grey. It is a colour combination that makes me think of French châteaux. And drawing on that association, I began to use gold in collages and on fabrics. Its attraction is not just about colour — there is the reflective quality to it as well.' By the time her furniture and fabrics have been dipped in gold dust, the result is not just fairy-tale, it is also pure glamour.

Stepping from a dusty London street into the jewel-box interior of her apartment-cum-studio, you could be forgiven for thinking that you were in Paris and that this was a couturier's salon. Gorgeous materials are flung across a large worktable, ready to be cut and sewn into harem-style cushions or else hung on a beribboned clothes rail. Ornate Venetian mirrors and

Quartermaine was inspired by this picture of massed glass on a mantelpiece, the tarnished mirror providing a misty after-image of layers of translucency, as though she were looking into a pool of still water disturbed only by the occasional ripple. The eerie ambiguity of hollow wicker mannequins and tailors' dummies also fascinates her.

crystal sconces float on the walls while curious wicker mannequins turn this way and that in silent conversation.

Everywhere there are boxes, pressed into service as an elegant alternative to drawers and storage space. They give the impression that their owner has been on some extravagant shopping trip, while the shoes and scent bottles scattered around suggest that you have stumbled into the boudoir of an exquisitely dressed nomad.

Quartermaine is an artist who sees life in close up, and when she looks at something its surface comes into sharp focus. For her, a plaster wall scrawled with graffiti is as worthy of interest as a canvas covered in oil paint. 'I like things in which you can see the layers of history — little pieces of wallpaper or the last vestiges of a fresco. I like very old chairs with ripped fabrics and old embroidery.'

Graffiti on a wall might seem a strange form of inspiration, but the words and scratches serve to break up the flatness. They become part of the wall's textural quality. The immediacy of the marks also appeals to Quartermaine — they represent moments captured in time. If you squint at these random scrawls, you could be looking at a Jean Cocteau letter, or a page torn from one of Picasso's notebooks.

A wonderfully romantic sofa, the pile as soft as a lioness' paw, the sunlight lending the velvet a silvery sheen, can also inspire.

'I remember the day that I first saw Noelle Höeppe's photograph of that sofa in *Vogue Decoration*,' she recalls. 'It immediately drew me in. I wanted to know everything about the room that the sofa was in.'

So finely tuned is Quartermaine's eye that when she looks at that old, marked velvet, or a piece of paper the colour of butterscotch with crease lines criss-crossing the surface, she begins to make connections and finds inspiration for new things in her work. 'The cracked surface of such paper is something I want to capture in my fabrics,' she says. 'It is curious how something as incidental as a piece of brown paper or a photograph in a magazine can send your work off in a new direction.'

But there are other influences that are more conventional. The decorative traditions of the French, for example: 'I adore France and I've always been inspired by those classical eighteenth-century and early nineteenth-century French interiors. The rooms are so restful, very composed, very formal.' This empathy with French style can be seen in her choice of Louis XVI furniture. But history needs to be updated, so whereas château-style, with furniture placed around the edge of a room, is all about formality, Quartermaine uses a more modern approach. Chairs are grouped in conference, small tables are at hand to take that coffee cup or book, the classic damask is replaced by her own more fluid designs.

Carolyn Quartermaine's vision makes almost no distinction between the graffiti-like marks on an antique velvet sofa and the distressed surface of graffiti-covered walls.

She is also drawn to the purity of Scandinavian interiors. The manor houses of Sweden used all the elements of French style and craftsmanship, but somehow pared them down until the lines became simpler, the dimensions more comfortable and the fabrics more utilitarian. 'I like the way that Swedish rooms look as if the colour has been bleached out of them,' she says. 'They borrowed a lot from the French — the shapes and styles — but in using plainer materials, the look became less ornate.'

Quartermaine likes to storm through different disciplines — painting, printing, writing and collaging, always finding different ways of expressing her artistic vision. This magpie mentality is a very twentieth-century way of working, and one which Quartermaine revels in. So, whether she is art directing a photography session or painting and creating textiles, everything for her is simply part of the process of making art. But there is a defining element to all these different media. She uses collage, both to produce dreamily lyrical pictures and as a jumping-off process for her other work. 'Collage informs all my work,' she says. 'It's the way I like to approach things, sitting at a table, cutting papers and fabrics, playing with paints.'

All the fabrics and papers that she uses are pure couture — almost every scrap and fragment is custom-dyed and printed — which leads to work of quite extraordinary texture and depth. Looking into the surface of *Lettres Impériales*, for example, you can just make out snatches of gold script on leaves of orange- and peach-coloured silk, fat scrolls or gilded dolphins diving into a line of poetry. The effect is as if someone

Quartermaine is drawn to artists' studios: 'we always view work in galleries; that is, clean spaces. It would be so wonderful to see the creative process as well as understanding the finished piece of work.' In her own studio, the whole space is transformed into an ever-changing collage of ideas, textures and colours.

The artist's world in close up. Although the choices may appear random, objects are put together with a discriminating eye and a magpie's love of sparkling treasures. Lengths of organza, in shades of caramel, lilac and aquamarine, are hung about a table like maypole ribbons, creating a cloth that moves in the breeze. A mass of cut-crystal chandelier drops and glass balls becomes a drift of bubbles. Steel buttons on a card are transformed into a display case of costly gems. The cool simplicity of a moment in Quartermaine's home echoes the chaste elegance of the eighteenth-century Scandinavian interiors she admires.

had dropped an old and precious folio of letters and billets-doux and then quickly bundled them back together again. The whole thing is irresistible; you can't help but be drawn into this web of shadowy words and images that conceal as much as they reveal. And as you read the poetry snaking across the collage, you begin to make out yet more clues on this romantically tattered and distressed surface.

The apparent spontaneity of Quartermaine's collages belies a strict editing process. 'By paring everything down, you are led to create a relationship between objects, textures and colours.' Imagine a bag of fabric pieces being spilled onto the floor: a flower print will fall next to a striped piece of silk, a cappuccino-coloured damask will lie on top of some blue *Toile de Jouy* and all of it will be set off by a length of gold embroidery. 'Then you start to play with those elements,' says Quartermaine, 'exploring the possibilities.' The result is

romantic, glamorous and sensual, a body of work that has such an alluring narrative quality that it seems to be part of some half-forgotten history that exists only to tease and tantalize, sending out messages from another world.

Rooms, too, are treated as if they were a collage come to life. 'Looking through my room now, I can see a length of silver embroidery next to a lilac, handpainted silk. Happy accidents like this start me thinking.' Gradually, her finely edited details build up into a total look, the two dimensions of a collage becoming the three dimensions of an interior.

The legendary fashion diva Diana Vreeland said that style has nothing to do with good taste. Style is about surprise, about taking things one stage further than good taste might be thought to allow. So in Quartermaine's apartment, what passes for ornamentation is slightly unorthodox. Instead of the usual array of glass, china and

photograph frames, there are scent bottles, handbags, and glass jars filled with powders and potions and adorned with faded gold labels. Sitting on a chair is a pile of note-paper tied with a flowered ribbon; a card of diamanté buttons is propped on the ledge of a white marble fireplace; and pretty ribbons trail onto the floor from a tabletop that has been piled up with crystal chandelier drops.

Diana Vreeland also once said that elegance is refusal, and looking at Quartermaine's rigorously edited interiors, you can see that she agrees. Everywhere you look, her eye has already eliminated the fuss and the frou-frou, paring things right down to what she calls 'the best details'. And what might those details be? 'Pin a piece of paper on a wall and place a bergère chair in front, hang lovely fabric at the windows, add a good floor and flowers . . . maybe that is all you really need in any room for it to be beautiful,' she says.

Chandeliers in an Indian temple, wrapped in dyed and faded cottons, provide Carolyn Quartermaine with inspiration for wrapping her own chandelier and draping her bed in sheer white cotton, hung from a simple pole. Wrapped and layered, draped and veiled, the fabrics create their own sense of mystery, while the crisp sunlight and vivid freshness of the colour transport this London scene to some Mediterranean shore.

Of course, this pure approach demands that you look closely and pay attention; in a world as intimate and personal as this, the positioning of an object is just as important as the choice of the object itself. In Quartermaine's sitting room, the ice blue of a card of buttons is picked up by the length of silk hung at the window. The crystal teardrops of a chandelier are reflected in the mirror-mosaic table. Free-flowing shapes like spirals, curlicues and scrolls are everywhere, from the words '*Toile Royale*' printed on the cover of a notepad to the choice of a curvy crystal wall sconce or the snaky legs of a table. The palette is all greys, blues, pinks and mauves. Light is refracted and reflected through crystal drops, mirrored surfaces and semi-sheer fabrics. Walking through a room as pretty as this conjures up images of childhood stories — you could be walking through Alice's looking glass into another world.

Although the look seems spontaneous, the working process to achieve that look is rigorous. Quartermaine has worked hard to create her world. She knows immediately whether a chair or a piece of furniture is 'her', seeing past the chipped paint or ripped embroidery to the bare bones beneath. 'I make visual choices every day that I never question,' she explains. 'I can look at something and know whether or not it is right in an instant.' It could be flair, it could be discipline, it could be that incredibly well-trained eye, but Quartermaine is very sure about what makes up the elements of her style. 'If you know what your taste is, then you have to develop it as much as you can and not be tempted to mix it up too much. You have to go with what you are. I feel very strongly that my apartment is an expression of me, of what is important to me — where I have been and what I have done. Certainly it expresses who I am now.'

Colour

'I THINK THAT EVERYONE HAS A COLOUR SENSE THAT IS ALL THEIR OWN. THE COLOURS THAT I PUT AROUND ME NOW ARE SIMILAR TO THE PAINTINGS THAT I DID WHEN I WAS A CHILD. OF COURSE, MY KNOWLEDGE HAS BEEN EXPANDED THROUGH TRAINING AND ART SCHOOL, BUT MY EYE FOR COLOUR, MY PALETTE, MY TASTE . . . I FEEL I WAS BORN WITH IT.

'I GO THROUGH PERIODS IN MY WORK THAT ARE COLOUR-LED. A LONG BLUE PERIOD MIGHT THEN LEAD ME TO BOLD, VERY STRONG COLOURS, WHICH IN TURN MIGHT MAKE ME WANT TO WORK WITH WHITES, GREYS AND GOLDS. PALE COLOURS CAN BE CLEANSING. BUT THEN THE HUNGER FOR NEW COLOURS RETURNS. I DON'T THINK THAT YOU CAN SURVIVE FOR VERY LONG ON A PALETTE THAT IS PREDOMINANTLY BEIGE.'

Taking a cue from nature: the lustrous sheen and
pearl-grey-and-rainwater colours of a collection of shells can
be replicated by a simple still-life of artists' materials.

'I like colours that are alive, that are layered, that seem to contain themselves, and more.'

Quartermaine loves the way water holds colour, and changes colour so rapidly. In a still-life inspired by notions of transparency and layers of blue, she takes heirloom glasses and a paper coaster picked up as a souvenir from a wedding on Cap Ferrat, and mixes them with watery shades to recreate the essence of the layered colours to be found in the sea.

Watching the way that Quartermaine works with colour — in fact, the way she works *through* colour — is to see much of the essence of her artistic vision exposed. Everything that fascinates her, interests her or sets her off on a flight of fancy can be traced back to her enjoyment of colour and to her highly personal colour syntax.

She pilfers crazy colour combinations from the world of high fashion as easily as picking out a riotous mix of hues from a traditional English flower border. She is like a conjurer, mixing tangerine with lilac, emerald green with copper, citrus yellow with hot pink, in a brazen display of colourful chic.

'I like very strong colour,' she says, 'colour with spirit and verve.' And it is this appetite that sets her apart. But she also reveals an eye for subtle gradations. There is nothing oppressive about the colours she picks, and the tonal make-up is exact. But if she knows how to play with vibrant colour, she likes equally to play with pale tones. 'It's true that some of the colours I like are so pale that it is as if all the colour has been bleached out,' admits Quartermaine. 'I like them because they are so ethereal and romantic.'

And now she is falling under the spell of silver. 'In fact, it is not a colour that I have been drawn to in the past. It is difficult to print with, and it can look so cold. But now I am beginning to experiment with it. I love it for its reflective quality and the way that it looks so good with oyster-coloured satin, or even with a strong pink.'

She thinks about colour in a refreshingly upbeat way. For her there are no colour wheels, no charts, no theorizing, just her own intensely personal and emotional response to the colours around her. Seeing a group of shimmering sea-shells might lead to a modern reworking of silvers, pearls and whites in an idiosyncratic still-life of galvanized metal buckets, diamanté tiaras and a lead-coloured table-cloth. All colours are evocative, and these pale translucents are no exception.

For Quartermaine, for whom colours are as descriptive as words, such a selection of colours is reminiscent of the 1930s and the ideal of the decorator Syrie Maugham, who sought to banish colour from chic apartments in her craze for all-white rooms. It sparked off the vogue for white fur rugs and bleached French salon furniture, and in turn, the fashion for wearing bias-cut satin slip-dresses and for placing diamanté clips in the hair.

Able to isolate colours, to see their historical and artistic resonances Carolyn Quartermaine then spins them off in some startling new direction. When she does something as innocent as placing a cheap blue plastic bag, behind lollipops covered in an aquamarine-and-white scrolled foil, so that the light shines through it, there is nevertheless a colour-inspired association driving the choices she makes. 'For me, this blue is like a drink. It is the colour of sea-water in the Mediterranean, a colour of sea so tempting that I can never resist diving into it — totally immersing myself in it. When the light came through that bag, it immediately made me think of the sea, of the slow lapping of shallow water onto a sandy beach.'

She can evoke a sandy cove, parasols and the heavy heat of the Mediterranean with her choice of transparent, watery blues. Even the map of Crete, pulled

out of her box of potential collaging papers on a whim, has its place in intensifying the seaside feeling. And it is because her sense of colour, light and texture is so refined that she can play such convincing visual tricks. She can actually make you see a whole beach in a blue plastic bag.

But if these are considered 'hot' blues, Quartermaine is equally adept at turning down the heat — at using blue to recreate the pure lines and the pale colours of a classic Swedish interior. 'I like the particular combination of greys, blues and whites that was used in Swedish decoration,' she says.

She is also drawn to the simplicity of the materials that the Swedish used in late eighteenth-century interiors. 'The way that they managed to achieve interiors of such delicacy using canvas, painted wood and linen. For me those checked

Historic colour: Quartermaine can achieve an instant ageing effect by layering paint and silk. Painted paper flaking from the inside of a lined cupboard might inspire her to collage sections of printed, rusted silk onto a door. Flat colour is not for her: instead she will play with it, making it richer, lifting it with washes of paint and the texture of silk, enjoying the contrast of 'dirty' grey and fresh colour, and echoing the patina of age.

Colour is all about balance —
knowing what to do with very
strong colour, how to contain it
and just when to stop. Red,
for example, looks good when
it is balanced by 'dirtier' or
neutral colours. Quartermaine's
'French Script' design on
the sofa, over-printed on a red
and bordeaux stripe, gives
depth to the colour, while the
stripes give structure. Offset
by gold, red takes on historical
resonances, reminiscent of
imperial grandeur.

blue-and-white linens have a timeless, appealing freshness about them,' she explains.

But what she really loves about those interiors is the sense of their unfinishedness. This has something to do with the plainness of the decoration and the restricted palette that was favoured because it made the most of the fine, clear northern light. 'When you think of a classic French interior,' she continues, 'you imagine a room that is very "decorated", with exquisitely rich embroidered silk on the chairs and lengths of silk damask on the walls. But what I really like in French châteaux is the grey paint on the shutters and the way sheer fabric is hung at the windows. In Sweden, those pared-down elements are all you get. It's so pure, so incredibly simple.'

Of course, Quartermaine's taste for Swedish colours is exact. When she talks about Sweden, she is referring to the Gustavian era, in the late eighteenth century (between 1770 and 1790) and the decorative style which flourished there. For her, it is a style typified by a country house called Ekensberg, where the interiors are so pure that you can sense chasteness.

Again, it is not just the colours that attract her. True, she can accurately split up a scheme into its chromatic components, but she sees more. She sees the *quality* of the colours. 'It is to do with the different finishes of them. Those dead-flat pale colours that are extremely beautiful when they are put against the high gloss of a white-tiled stove or reflected in chandelier drops and pier-glasses.' As she explains the plot of this colour narrative, you suddenly notice that her nails are painted in pearl-white nail varnish, the shade of frozen snowdrops.

Someone else might be content to isolate the elements they are drawn to and then copy them faithfully in some slavish homage, but that is not Quartermaine's style. While she keeps the colours and the exact historical reference clearly in her mind, she nevertheless begins to play with the elements, the palette, in her own artistic update on a decorative style. She takes the specifics of, say, Swedish-style blue-grey paintwork, but adds a wash of turquoise and a piece of rusted turquoise silk for depth. The effect is luscious without being heavy or overdone, perhaps due to the transparency of the fabric and the casual way in which it is collaged onto the door panel. So too, the blue-and-white checks that are so common on Swedish chairs are translated to a silk ticking-stripe. It is enough to suggest a particular historical style, without being over-literal.

'Of course, the quality of the light makes an enormous difference in the way colours are seen,' Quartermaine says. 'They can look punchy and modern in a clear light, but certainly if the light is softer

and more diffused, it will give a more historical and romantic feel to the colours that are being used.'

She is very aware of the historical associations of the colours she picks, and the signals she sends out just by choosing certain combinations. She rarely uses red, for example, but when she does, that use is self-assured. 'The best red to copy,' said Diana Vreeland, whose life was a passion for finding the perfect shade, 'is the colour of any child's cap in a Renaissance painting.' In fact, Vreeland was so in thrall to red that she did up her apartment like a glamorous carmine cell, kept her skin kabuki-pale to offset the flame red of her lipstick and had a weakness for wearing matador jackets.

'Red is attractive, quite literally,' says Quartermaine. 'The eye can't help but be drawn to the woman in a red dress, the child running down the street in a red coat. Think of that powerful image in *Don't Look Now*.' She is speaking of Nicolas Roeg's chilling film of a Daphne du Maurier short story. Against the muted

tones of Venetian stone, plaster and grey waterways, Donald Sutherland and Julie Christie were dressed in muted woollens and tweeds, and yet all the way through the film, there is also the sense that a red warning light is winking on and off: here with a flash of geraniums against a wall, there with a red coat.

But then if the eye instinctively searches for and isolates red, it can also be calmed by it. Quartermaine is quite aware of the mood-altering qualities of the colours she is drawn to. 'There is this wonderful sense of comfort that you get when you sit in an entirely red room,' she muses, 'especially if the hangings are old and heavy.' She likes the way red carries so much history in its wake — the heavy swish of the cardinal's robe, the pomp and splendour of Napoleon's bedchamber.

There is a shade of burnt orange that she associates with Italy. 'Maybe it is because of the way orange absorbs light, you can't help but look at it and feel heat,' she says. Or perhaps it is because it is so reminiscent of the colour of old painted

Even an expanse of the brightest colour will cease to be overwhelming when given texture. Quartermaine's painted, silk-squared and papered canvases give the effect of an artist's palette magnified on the wall. The bold taffetas on a gilt chair are softened by placing it on a stone floor. Overleaf: Isolating patches of colour in a mass of silk bags hung on a neutral stone wall, Quartermaine keeps each colour distinct, allowing fresh relationships to emerge between them.

walls and stucco that she cannot see this colour without being reminded of Siena, Padua or any one of a hundred Italian towns. To intensify the architectural associations, she might use a vibrant shade of orange with more neutral browns and beiges. And because Quartermaine's associations with Italy are so strong, she will translate the colour to London in winter. 'I do like to paint my balcony in orange when it's cold,' she admits. 'Then, looking through the windows, with the black traces of the trees beyond, the balcony becomes a band of mouthwatering colour. It reminds me of the ices I had as a child, which, even as I was eating them, would melt all over my clothes, and in that memory orange also brings back the warmth of a really hot summer.'

She is always conscious of the effect colours have on other colours, how colour combinations can feed into a palette, creating different moods. 'Orange, when it is isolated — maybe in a bowl of fruit or a vase of roses in a room — has a very strong effect. But I am not sure that I would want a whole room painted that shade of orange,' she concedes. 'Maybe just a wall. But it is such a joyous colour and has this way of enriching other things. A piece of brown paper, for example, is made to look more precious by setting it off against orange.' She then goes on to note how texture also plays its part. 'Add a pinch of burnt umber to those vibrant shades of tangerine and orange, and suddenly there you are in Italy, where the surface of a wall has been scratched or worn away until the stone colour is revealed beneath.'

One would hardly be surprised to discover that what interests Quartermaine is the point where colours meet and mix. 'There is a scene in the film *Indiscreet* that I love,' she says. It is evidence of how her eye will always instinctively gravitate to the voluptuous mix of colour and pattern that has been such a strong element in her work. While others might be watching Cary Grant and Ingrid Bergman go through their paces, Quartermaine is

Some colours add richness by means of subliminal associations. A day bed is given a slick of Empire grandeur through gilding and dressing in dramatic aubergine silk.

captivated by the film set. 'In Bergman's apartment there is a set of huge prints either side of the fireplace. The whole apartment is just perfect, but these pictures are particularly striking because the mounting boards are all different colours. The effect is startling, like an oversized mosaic on a plain wall.'

In consequence, when Quartermaine takes a dazzling selection of silk drawstring bags and hangs them on the wall, she knows exactly what she is up to. And the effect is ravishing, like jellybeans in a jar or looking deep into one of Klimt's flower paintings. 'This is my version of a Klimt flower garden, but on a wall. In looking at those paintings, the dots and dashes which make up the flower heads look like drops of pure colour.'

When colour is this headstrong, she doesn't try to tame or fix it by painting it in broad expanses on walls or floors. She has no commitment to an overall colour scheme, instead allowing colour the freedom to roam. It is an approach that shows the beauty in having drops of strong, intense and distinct colour placed against a plain background. You cease to see the colours in isolation and instead watch as relationships begin to form between the strongly contrasting shades, and textures are thrown into sharp relief.

But, of course, colour can be just as intoxicating when it is taken straight rather than mixed into a cocktail. Intense shades of grape, aubergine and cassis, enriched with swirls of gilt script, look elegant and refined when set against the dull grey of beautiful panelling. The matt quality of the paint and the floorboards allow the

Lilac, for Quartermaine, is the colour that calls up the strongest emotional response. A springtime colour, serene and fresh, it shares the fleeting quality of water, sky and glass. Discreet and ambiguous, it is immensely versatile. An artichoke head appears to grow out of a paper crown, (originally wrapped around a fez in a Marrakesh bazaar), which provides a neutral backdrop. The tea-stained colour of the dummy, on which two lilac scrolls have been pinned in a neat reworking of Man Ray's famous photograph, provides a similarly understated foil.

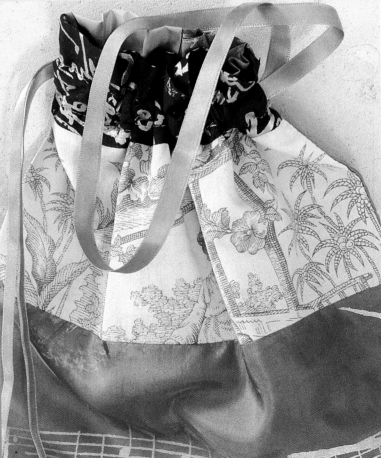

richness of the colour to come through. In a sense, it is a scheme that allows colour junkies to indulge their craving for intense experience without sensory overload, and as such it has a wonderfully modern sensibility to it all.

Just as she rarely puts acres of flat, intense colour onto walls, preferring instead to leave them pale and use strong colour on chairs or banners, Quartermaine creates separate pools of intensity in different places around a room. And despite her soft spot for eighteenth-century-inspired furniture, it is this treatment of a space that makes it so clearly contemporary.

Even when Quartermaine limits a room to two main colours, such as cassis and grey, she achieves a cool and classic set piece, but one that is undoubtedly of the present. The air of refinement comes from the fact that any potential for Napoleonic excess — the love of rich textiles and saturated colour — has been distilled to just two tones. Instead of an overbearing array of splendour, there is instead a haunting evocation, a suggestion of mood. It is as if the artist had chosen to suggest an idea through a line drawing, say, rather than a fully painted, and highly coloured, canvas.

Of course, if Quartermaine were forced to choose any single colour over another, it would probably be a certain shade of blue-pink lilac. She resists any attempts to label it her 'signature colour', but admits that it is a recurring theme in her work. 'Lilac is the key,' she says of her favourite tone. 'It is elegant, serene, calming, spiritual and cleansing.' And mood-altering. 'I am

always very happy to have lilac around me, it is just so beautiful.'

She applauds the way lilac cleans up other colours, looks good not only when it is at its most transclucent — for example, as a piece of tissue paper — but also in more intense incarnations, such as in a dye-saturated length of silk. It looks fabulous with steel colours, and it is freshening with whites. It is luxurious with gold and entrancing as glass.

Her love of lilac, her fascination with this one shade, confirms her unique response to colour. Whether it is the fragility, transparency, or density of a colour that she notices, she simply cannot observe colour without the quality of it (over and above its chromatic make-up) affecting what she sees. And it is this acute analysis that enables her to play with the layering and juxtaposition of shades and tints in such an arresting way. She might apply the faintest wash of aquamarine to a scarred

concrete wall, allowing the broken surface to show through the colour, or she might have silks dyed with such an intensity that they look as if they have been dipped into pure pigment. And then she might mix the two types of colour together in a perfectly balanced way.

'There is no acidity in the colours that I choose,' she explains. 'And where I use strong colour there always has to be a balance. It might be no more than a contrasting band of piping around the seat of a chair, but there is always a restraining element.'

You cannot be around her work for very long before you realize that Quartermaine sees the world through highly sensitive eyes: sensitive to the light, to subtle gradations in tone, and also to texture. She has an affinity with those soft-washed greys of driftwood and old stone, and the sparkly blue reminiscent of the Mediterranean in high summer. If she changes the texture of these colours — by

distressing the surface, scratching them, scoring them, dropping blobs of gold onto them — then these same tones, borrowed from nature, evoke a sense of romance and history. That same driftwood grey becomes the grey of panelling in a French château, while the deep blue of seawater looks as though it has been snipped from the hem of an imperial cape. 'Texture is so important when I am thinking about colour,' she explains. 'When you break up the colour, you allow it to breathe. When you paint a wall, and have the courage to leave its surface imperfections, it can look stunning.'

Quartermaine also speaks of what she calls 'fragile colour'. 'It is the colour you get when you hang a length of silk organza at a window. Imagine it. Maybe it is silver or lavender in colour; you look through the fabric and the world takes on a slightly different hue. Or you can see fragile colour in the way light

The moodiest blues. Colours can recreate our fantasies. With satins and sheers, blue silks become more than just a canopy to dress a bed, turning it into something rather like a kitsch version of a gypsy caravan. The materials can be inexpensive — the sense of abundance comes from the freshness of the colour, the play of shine and sheer. Together, by some mysterious alchemy, modest individual elements conspire to create an atmosphere of extravagant romance. The freshest colours are those found in flower petals, or the drift of a field of lavender. The green stems of the lavender and the stamens of the passion flower look as if they have been dipped in pure pigment.

Hot colour, clean colour, can appear most exuberant when mixed in carefully balanced, though apparently audacious, combinations. Whatever the surface — from lampstands to seating — Carolyn Quartermaine revels unashamedly in the full potential of bold colour. A swathe of fuchsia silk is placed with strong lilacs and even brighter yellows. Citrus shades of lime and lemon are used with confidence to slice through shocking pinks. Strong, sharp colour is tempered by a more delicate shade, so that it retains its vibrancy without overpowering, and larger expanses of discreet colour are used to balance more concentrated splashes of intense brilliance.

'When looking at anything, the first point of reference for me will be its colour.'

comes through rose petals. Perhaps the best way to describe fragile colour,' she adds, 'is to think of looking up into a faded silk parasol held above your head in full sunlight.'

She sees these washes and whispers of colour as entirely separate shades from the more saturated tones. Listening to her speak, you realize that maybe this is why her take on colour is more multi-faceted, more interesting, and more beautiful than so much else on offer. It comes from her completely emotional response to the world around her, a world tempered by an eye trained in fine art and an intense appreciation of historical and architectural associations.

Colour contrasts: containing and contrasting expanses of sharp colour with a thin line of piping in an equally vibrant colour has the effect of framing chairs and cushions as though they were pictures. Two bands of lilac define the yellow of a chair seat and pick up the soft brush-stroked shade used on the fabric, while golden yellow edges a cushion of fuchsia taffeta.

Shape

'YOU CAN LOVE CERTAIN COLOURS, BUT COLOUR IS NOT WHAT DEFINES YOUR TASTE. SHAPE DEFINES YOUR TASTE BECAUSE OF WHAT IT FORCES YOU TO EXCLUDE. IF YOU ARE DRAWN TO FLOWING LINES, TO SCROLLS, TO CERTAIN SHAPES OF CHAIR, FOR EXAMPLE, IMMEDIATELY THERE IS MUCH THAT WILL NOT INTEREST YOU. AND IN THAT PROCESS OF THE EYE RECOGNIZING WHAT IT LIKES, YOUR TASTE IS DEFINED.

'EVER SINCE I WAS A CHILD, SINCE DOLLS' HOUSE DAYS, I HAVE ALWAYS BEEN ATTRACTED TO THE SAME THINGS — I THINK I HAVE AN APPRECIATION OF FINE, DELICATE, I SUPPOSE SOME PEOPLE WOULD CALL THEM FEMININE, SHAPES. THE WHOLE PROCESS FOR ME IS QUITE INTUITIVE. AND YET THIS INTUITION IS AT THE VERY HEART OF EVERYTHING THAT I DO.'

Driftwood may be as elegant as the carved frame of a classic French chair, and both may have the same qualities as a delicate piece of sculpture. Overleaf: fine proportions create a sense of space, and mouldings add structure: what more does a room need except a few skilfully chosen pieces?

In this decorative world, there are no straight lines. Instead, every object, every line, seems to have been stroked into a curve or a scroll as if it had been drawn with an italic pen. For shape that is a little less hard-edged, the light shining through barely-there silk produces shadows that look as if they have been drawn with a charcoal stick and then smudged slightly. Choosing objects of a similar shape, or with similar surface decoration, is a neat piece of editing. The stitching on a length of embroidery might echo the curve of a metal table, which picks up the details of painted upholstery and carving on the wooden frame of a chair. Looked at in this way, furniture can be seen as a two-dimensional line pushed into three.

When Carolyn Quartermaine turns her attention to the subject of shape, there are very few compromises — and even fewer straight lines. Perched on one of a pair of her favourite French gilded chairs ('I have never found a chair that is a better shape than these'), she theorizes on the relationship between proportion, sculptural form and taste. 'Everything comes down to shape; it is the most important consideration. For me, the way the light hits crystal drops on a chandelier is unimportant if the shape of the chandelier is wrong in the first place.' And she points to her own finely wrought chandelier dancing above her head to illustrate her point. 'Shape is the soul of something, it animates things that have no life. Shape is the structure on which everything else depends.'

Perhaps it is the sumptuousness of the colours she chooses, and the seductiveness of her work, that make it all too easy to ignore the discipline and rigour that goes into what she has achieved. It is in understanding the way she can choose objects and furniture without any hesitation — the selection process that occurs before colour has even been thought about — that you see just how refined her taste is. And this selection process has only to do with shape. There is the lazy curve of the neck of a favourite scent bottle, the scroll of a treble clef, the rounded dome of a 1960s moulded plastic stool that she has

chosen to re-cover in swirly embroidered silk from India. Design pedants might balk, but Quartermaine is dancing to an altogether more lyrical tune. Looking at the things with which she has chosen to surround herself, you realize that the same shapes are repeated everywhere, similar forms are echoed, and fine lines appear in duplicate and triplicate, gorgeously gilded. 'You have to be so uncompromising about shape,' she says as she explains why she finds the proportion of her English nineteenth-century carved-wood sofa so pleasing. 'Shape demands the highest purity. No uncertainty, no fudging.'

She loves the balance that proportion and shape seem to impose on an interior. 'It is something that I notice a lot in Italian rooms. The proportions are so exquisite, there seems to be more space. There might be a fresco on the wall, a stone floor and plain linen hanging at the doorways. It is all *very* simple. Given the

right elements, I would love to live in that purer way.' She applauds the near-empty room, as it allows her to focus on shape all the more. Having one lampshade, one chair, one bed, means that she can see clearly the interplay of each piece with the others, the relationships that evolve, the textures that echo each other. But the rhythms should not be too exact. Quartermaine does not like elements to be repeated too literally. 'I like things to be a little bit impromptu, a little bit wayward.' So much so that when she was completing a set of collages recently, she fell in love with the way that a spool of lime-green silk thread had fallen in a loop on her work. She painstakingly glued the thread into the chance pattern until it danced across her collage. Many of her fabrics are designed with such elements of randomness. 'It gives me a buzz. I do not like things to look too planned, too formulaic,' she explains.

For Quartermaine shape is revolutionary. It can change the way we see, and alter the way in which we respond to the world around us. Quite simply, shape reorganizes our space, and with it our consciousness. Architecture is just one example of how our horizons can be manipulated. Coming out of the First World War, for example, the move towards Modernism with its reductive lines and lack of ornamentation spoke of a

Even very disparate objects have a relationship if you are looking purely at shape. Here, the stiffened lace of antique shoes finds echoes in the pattern of a fine metalwork balustrade on the rue de Rivoli in Paris.

world where affluence would depend on mass production. In fashion, designers will first search for a silhouette, refining and reworking the shape of each new collection, only then using fabrics to exaggerate or complement their work. Madeleine Vionnet, the French couturière, experimented with very pure-looking shapes, cut on the bias, in a feat of technical virtuosity. To further accentuate these fluid forms, she would use layers of semi-transparent sheers, or drapes of silk satin.

In 1947, Christian Dior unveiled the exaggerated form of his 'New Look' — all cinched waists and padded hips — which lent women's bodies a new silhouette and in doing so caused an uproar in a society still constrained by post-war austerity. He called this first collection 'Corolla', taking the pleated, petal shapes of a flower and hanging them on a stiffly corseted frame. It was his reaction to the stiffness of war-time fashion, in which suits and dresses looked as inflexible as armour. He expressed it like this: 'In December 1946, as a result of the war and the uniforms, women still looked and dressed like Amazons. But I designed clothes for flower-like women, with rounded shoulders, full feminine busts, and hand-span waists above enormous spreading skirts.' In an unconscious homage to Christian Dior's aesthetic, Quartermaine chose to call one of her lampshade designs

'Bluebell'. These shades are reminiscent of a 1940s cocktail dress; the comparison is charming.

She is as precise in the silhouette she adopts when *she* is getting dressed as she is about the shapes she designs to top her impossibly fine, gilded standard lamps. 'I don't like baggy clothes,' she says. 'I like things that are cut and that fit close to the body. I love designers like Givenchy and Balenciaga — those elegant, classic forms that are so pure and simple.' And if she does not always feel like wearing a Givenchy *tailleur*, she will satisfy her need for cut and proportion by watching Audrey Hepburn in *Sabrina Fair* or *Charade*. 'Have you ever noticed how clothes look so much better in films?' she says. 'It is when you are watching a movie that you can really concentrate on the *form* of a costume.' And here she adds, 'In real life, when I walk into a room, it is rare that I am ever really struck by the

shape of someone in the same way that I would be struck by an actress in a movie. In real life, it is more to do with details: the way a brooch is pinned, or the choice of a necklace.'

That finely tuned eye is working over-time again. In one blink it seems to take in what many never see, and it is as if she sees through the surface of things to the structure beneath. For example, while everyone else is sorting and organizing their furniture by period, or maybe by colour, Quartermaine uses an entirely separate set of criteria. There is a key to the way she places so many disparate objects, from different eras and different countries, so confidently together to create the Quartermaine-style — and that key is shape. 'I know instantly if one piece of furniture is compatible with another. It does not matter if it is antique or modern, even of rusted metal. She can strip a chair with her eyes, quickly take in its form, remove extraneous detail until she sees through to that all-important skeletal form. She is the girl with the X-ray eyes. It is the same with my clothes,' she adds. 'It is easy, I just know.'

Her early training in sculpture was an asset. 'When I first went to art school, I started in the sculpture department. I loved making shapes, working with solid form. It was only because I could not do without colour that I moved across to

'I look for shape that dances with movement and irresistibly draws the eye to it.'

painting.' While she no longer sculpts, this training further disciplined her eye to the point that, for her, a carved Louis XVI chair has all the qualities of a piece of sculpture. 'I definitely prefer Louis XVI furniture to Louis XV,' she laughs. 'The legs are better.'

There is nothing rigid about her preferred shapes. After all, this is the girl who gilded piles of imperfectly shaped papier-mâché hearts, purely because she was entranced by the look of them; who cut hearts from paper and applied them to her collages ('After all, what else is a heart, but two scrolls?'). These motifs turn up time and time again on her fabrics, each one a little different from the next, but all looking as if they had been quickly hand-drawn and then cut out. 'I adore shapes that are suggestive of other things,' she says by way of explanation. 'I don't like things that are too perfect, too finished.'

Shape is about sensuality. Lightness, grace and an almost drinkable fluidity characterize the shapes that Carolyn Quartermaine creates, and those that she is drawn to. Previous pages: couture lamp-shades reminiscent of exaggerated flower shapes, pert Audrey Hepburn hats and extravagantly flounced skirts.

que chaque planche doit...

Quoique ... planches s'élèvent jusqu'à la partie supérieure de la caisse, assez ... elle-même pour surmonter les eaux moyennes ... ferme par ... horizontale jointure et calfatée l'espace compris entre ... couture supérieure des cours de moise.

... construire la caisse sur au dessus de l'enclave ... qu'elle ... occuper, on ... ce apparemment soutenu au moyen ... qu'elle ... reliés entre eux par de longues pièces de bois repo... sur ... les eaux.

Dans le premier cas on construisit préalablement un échafaud ... tour de l'emplacement de la pile, et c'est sur cet échafaud que reposent les semelles qui servent à contenir la ... et le lieage des pièces de charpente. Pour l'immerger, on la ... au moyen de caux en nombre suffisant, puis quand les ... sont enlevés, on la descend progressivement jusqu'à son immersion complète.

Quand la caisse ... construite sur un ... on peut l'amener ... ou construction au ... placement ... à l'eau où la ... de ... la ... ou ensuite au moyen de treuils disposée comme ... 1, 2, 7 et 8 ... que les bateaux qu'on ... la ... à la caisse ... du gravier en volume suffisant pour ... les bateaux ... une position horizontale.

Quel que ... ... qu'on ... le procédé d'em... il faut ... ... proportions nécessaires pour que ... aussi ...

... de 3 — ... sur le rocher ... de gravier dans les cuvettes ...

Lorsque le ... chaque avant l'im... mersion de la caisse, on est obligé de la faire avec grande

Simple shapes and things you can see through — whether swirls of metal on a window grille or classic café tables, flawed glass or a sculptural twist of vaporous fabric — fascinate Quartermaine and inform her vision. As with colour and light, shape in this world is evanescent and flighty, ever on the brink of suggesting — or becoming — something else.

And so there are the hand-drawn scrolls, the fine italic script that looks as if it has been applied to fabric or paper by a quill dipped in gold ink, and the elliptical shapes of her papier-mâché plates. 'Ovals are more satisfying than circles,' she says. 'And what I love about my plates is that they are slightly irregular ovals, the edges are almost fluted.' The other form she has been drawn to in the past is the cone, which she has made up in papier-mâché before painting or gilding the surface. She can take a geometric shape and, by virtue of its dimensions, the slight irregularities in the surface texture, and the colour, applied by hand, turn it into something inspirational.

She is adept at using shape to cast visual spells, or making things appear that normally we would not or could not see. Hence her elongated scrolls that seem to rise up and out of the open neck of a champagne bottle. 'They make me think of a wave of perfume,' she says, in order to explain why something so whimsical is so pleasing to the eye. 'I am always attracted to shapes that are lyrical; that flow in some way.'

This is why she was so painstaking about creating her striking lampshades. 'I wanted to make them look as if they were dancing,' she says, so she created a shape with a flirty sweep, which looks like the hem of a dress whooshed up and out by the swirl of a dancer's body. As is so often the case with her work, turning the mood — the feeling — into something more concrete took more than a little time. Creating the metal frame, the 'skeleton', took months in itself, and then finding someone with the skill and the patience to make up the shades was a lengthy and often frustrating process. Even now, dressing each metal body takes an age because each shade is fitted with specially cut panels of silk,

hand-stitched to the frame. (Most modern shades are glued.) To give some idea of the effort involved, she lets slip that each shade takes eight hours to stitch and bind. No wonder, then, that floating above their skinny stands, they look like a couturier's dream. 'I tend to put the plainer shades, like 'Pagoda', on a more elaborate stand, while 'Bluebell' looks good on something curlier.' Each of these intricate metal stands is forged for her and then silver- or gold-leaved depending on the effect she is trying to achieve.

Metalwork plays an important part in Quartermaine's work, especially when defining shape. Not only does she have all sorts of finely wrought pieces made up for her, to exacting specifications, but she is adept at nosing out the perfect antique metal console table or chair. Again, her choice is defined by elegance and refinement. 'I prefer simple nineteenth-century garden furniture. I am not keen

on anything from the 1950s because it is too gimmicky.' And then, thinking she can make you see her point more clearly, she adds, 'It is Miami, rather than French park.' Of course. But almost before you have grasped the fine distinctions she is making, she is off, describing what she loves so much about old metalwork. 'When I find a really good old metal chair, it is as if I can get all the things I love and more. First there is the elaborate shape. But then it will very often be rusted, so you can enjoy the wonderful interplay between texture and shape. And I love it when I can look through the scrolling metalwork of a garden chair and see fabric scrolls on the chair seat I have made, or maybe something of the wall beyond. It is the seeing through objects that is so beautiful.'

It also means that she can introduce quite large-scale pieces of furniture that do not shout and scream for attention.

The shapes are sexy, but they are discreet, too, and sometimes when they are made of glass, mirror, crystal and metal, they seem so light that they are barely there. Sheer fabrics and shadows add to this delicious floating sensation. She keeps just one bulb in her chandelier, for example, not because she is thrifty but because she loves 'the effect that one bulb has. The way it distorts all the scrolls and shapes of the chandelier into these extraordinary shadows on the wall. Everything becomes stretched and elongated; the patterns are so fantastic that it looks as though I have hung up the most beautiful sheer fabric on the walls.' And with the flick of a switch, she can erase it all.

She likes to stretch and distort, to play around with scale. 'I remember when Donna Karan saw one of my small collages and said, "I want to see this big!" Big to Donna meant the size of the whole wall.' And so they magnified Quartermaine's

Images and their echoes, like forms and their shadows, are central to Quartermaine's visual linking process, which delights in witty conceits. Carved and gilded flowers are given ethereal brush-stroked counterparts; scrolls forming a heart shape on a chair back find their complementary after-image cut from the same fabric and pinned to the wall behind.

design countless times over. 'What was so interesting was that the shapes looked even better, even more fluid, even more loose. I really became aware of a sense of movement.'

This says much about her attitude to shape. She likes shapes that look so fluid they could be sipped through a straw. And with everything she does, there is lightness of touch, as if her creations could defy gravity. There is always that upwards flick, that lack of heaviness. Observing Quartermaine's preferences is like looking at a line drawing, a fashion illustration maybe, where a suggestion of shape and form is more important than the shape itself. 'There are certain shapes that I find very elegant. I do not like anything that is hard-edged. That is why I love artists like Jean Cocteau; there was a quickness

of a mark, a star, a dash. Everything he did had that energy of a brushstroke.' She cites the French artist Christian Bérard, one of Cocteau's charmed circle, as preserving this same quality of unconscious mark-making. She continues, 'I love the idea that he would walk up to a piece of paper, draw something quickly, and then walk away again. But in that one act he captured the essence of the thing, the shape, the line. When you get a sense of movement and life, that is when mark-making is at its best.'

And that is what she is searching for: movement that has been trapped for an instant. 'It is true that I do not like objects to appear to be heavy. I want to keep everything fluid and full of movement.'

And what was her favourite game as a child? 'Musical statues, of course.'

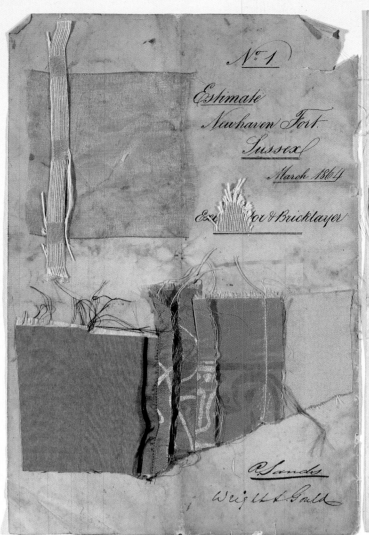

Nº 1

Estimate

Newhaven Fort.

Sussex

March 1864

Excavator & Bricklayer

R. Sands

Wright & Gold

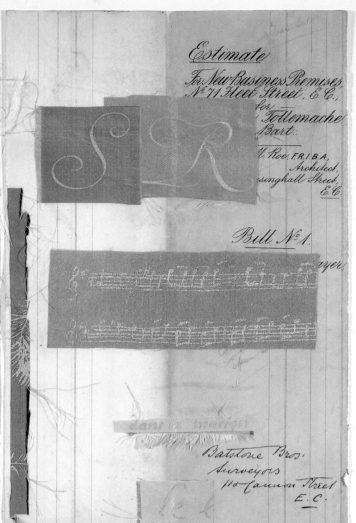

Estimate

For New Business Premises,
Nº 71 Fleet Street, E.C.,
for
Tollemache
Bart:

H. Roe, F.R.I.B.A,
Architect,
Lessinghall Street,
E.C.

Bill Nº 1.

Batstone Bros.
Surveyors
110 Cannon Street
E.C.

Continued £ 27607. 3. 11

abcdefghijklmnopqrstuvwxyz

She saw an ancient city park a que

893

7. 8. 10

238. 6. 3

Estimate   Newhaven Fort. Sussex

Fabric

'I NEVER SET OUT TO CREATE A TEXTILE COLLECTION. IN THE PAST I HAVE PRINTED UP LENGTHS OF SILK TO COVER CHAIRS AND THEN OVER-PRINTED AND PAINTED THEM. THERE ARE NO REPEAT PATTERNS ON THESE FABRICS, SO WHEN THEY WERE CUT INTO SMALL PANELS, EACH CHAIR SEAT WAS DIFFERENT.

'DESIGNING FABRICS ISN'T AN ABSTRACT THING. I ACHIEVE RESULTS BY WORKING THROUGH A PROCESS, BUT THERE IS NO FORMULA TO WHAT I DO. I MIGHT START OFF WITH ONE IDEA, BUT WHEN I PHYSICALLY START TO PRINT OR PAINT THE FABRICS, SOMETHING CAN TAKE ME OFF IN ANOTHER DIRECTION.'

*Sample-book or collage? Passementerie or still-life?
In Quartermaine's artful use of fabric, definitions slip and
slide with exhilarating ambiguity. Overleaf: sheer excess — the
soft opulence of the colours of silk taffeta is matched by
the languorous freedom with which it is used.*

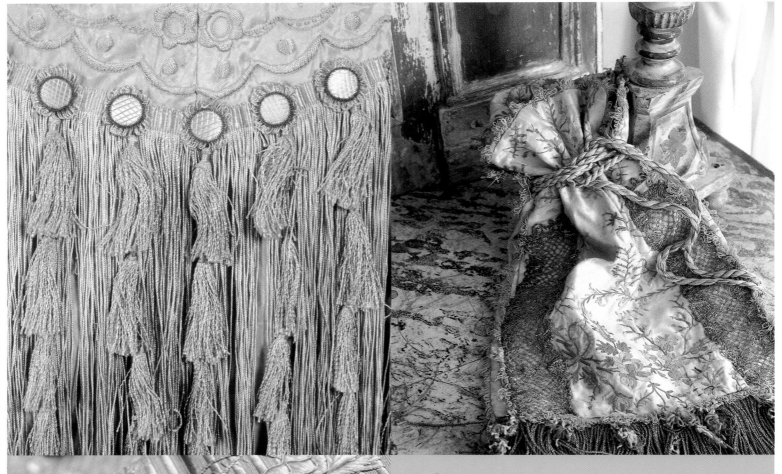

Shifts of scale and suggestions of
movement are important and exciting
to Quartermaine. Antique fringes and
tassels are like falling arabesques; a
section of embroidery viewed close-
up is pure ornament, reminiscent of
jewellery; a simple twist of multicoloured ribbons evokes baroque images
of Carnival in Venice, festive but
with darker undertones. Exquisitely
worked details, nonchalantly cut and
frayed strips, tangled or floating ribbons
— all display a delight in the feel and
mood of fabric.

When Quartermaine designs her textiles, she is very much hands-on. Rather than thinking up images and patterns in a vacuum and transferring from paper to fabric, she prefers to go through the whole printing process herself before the designs are made up in larger quantities. She feels strongly that it is only by seeing through each step in the printing, by being immersed in the physicality of it and carefully choosing inks and dyes and scales of pattern, that she can produce her best work.

She has convinced others that this is a good way to get results. 'When I did some fabric designs for Donna Karan,' she recalls, 'Donna wrapped herself entirely in black jersey and then we experimented. I stood with the collage patterns we wanted in the textile and taped them all around her body to see where they might fall. I could have done it as an abstract design at a table, but then I would have had no idea how that could translate to the body.'

Quartermaine is an artist who uses fabrics to cross boundaries — between fashion and interiors, history and the present day. Historical allusions trail behind her like the train of a mannequin's gown, but these allusions are stitched according to a very modern taste. She might paint roses onto lengths of ivory silk, with loose dashes of colour in homage to French Impressionism, but her roses are painted in a wonderful Yves Klein blue. And if she borrows the layout of an eighteenth-century silk weaver's pattern book, where fabric swatches are neatly lined up for comparison and easy selection, it is given a contemporary twist and turned into an album of her own designs.

Fashion seems to step off the catwalk and into her interiors as she takes metres of silk and whooshes them into a full-skirted ball gown. Her manner seems gloriously ad hoc — like Elsa Schiaparelli, who cocooned herself in crêpe de Chine when she had no money for a ball dress, Quartermaine is able to whip, pin, catch and tie fabrics into a tantalizing array of fashionable chic.

When she set about creating an intoxicating stage set of couture glamour in the stairwell of a fairy-tale French château, she knew that fabric was the most important element in creating the effect that she wanted. And so the bolts of fabric were rolled out, and metres and metres of shocking pink and green silk were slipped over the luscious curves of those wicker mannequins' hips to create each fantastical dress. 'And if you had walked up those stairs and looked down,' relates Quartermaine, 'you would have seen a train of ten metres of emerald silk falling down the stairs.'

Refreshingly, this excess is not about a vain show of status. Wanting some jewellery to complete such an outfit? Try silk spools strung into a necklace, the colours as rich as any glass beads. This is instant glamour, Quartermaine-style. 'There's something more satisfying about buying acres of cheap fabric and hanging it in great swathes,' she explains of her profligate use. 'Almost any material can look good if used in a spirit of generosity. It looks much more sumptuous than a small amount of expensive fabric made up in a tight and pompous way.'

Of course, she has always been fascinated with fabric. 'When I was studying fine art, I did a lot of collages using screen-printed textiles.' She then took to cutting the fabric

into strips and inter-weaving and layering them, all the while experimenting with colours and textures. She started applying dyes to her fabrics as if they were paintings, so producing unique lengths of cloth. And, in turn, other aspects of her work as a collage artist fed into her textile design. Patterning with script, for example, happened in the early days when she was designing papers for collages, but she later translated the writing to silk. 'I put the fabric on a chair, and that's when it all took off.' 'It' was 'French Script', one of the most desirable and instantly recognizable fabric designs of the 1980s — a design that took elements of French salons, *haute couture* and sheer glamour, and re-modelled all three for the decade.

Fabric is a fetish we can all associate with. The heavy drape of taffeta breaking on the floor, the messy jumble of ribbons spilling out of their box, the *fin-de-siècle* decadence of coloured silks. 'Silk is my favourite fabric,' says Quartermaine. 'It can be really vibrant . . . the colours are so true. And there is such luxury in the *shine*.'

But Quartermaine is not really interested in base fabrics, straight off the roll. She likes to cut them, dye them, slice them and sew them into her own magical creations. She is like a disc jockey who samples and edits

Antique spools of pastel-coloured silk thread in their original box, along with other tools of the couturier's trade, are kept for inspiration.

grooves and bass lines into new rhythms. So she will take her own fabrics and mix them with a combination of antique and contemporary textiles, Indian embroideries and classic chintzes, sheers and opaque gauzes, until she has covered her world in a luminous mosaic of shimmering cloth.

Even so, her appetite is hardly satisfied by a diet of pure fabric. She also feasts on accessories: silk reels, ribbons, cards of antique diamanté or mother-of-pearl buttons, all of which are as beguiling as the choice in a box of chocolates. Nestling in tissue, alongside gold thread, the colours of such skeins and passementerie are almost edible: marrons glacés, violet-creams and sugar-pinks. Such delicacies easily become the starting point for one of Quartermaine's silk throws. In fact, it's almost as if all the elements of her work are in just such a box, waiting to be unpacked. The label on a roll of ribbon looks as if it will be incorporated into one of her collages, and the patterning on the box of silk and cotton spools looks as restrained as the nineteenth-century, paper-bound novels that lie scattered around her apartment. But such elements are more than inspiration; they are treated as ornaments in their own right. They are the tools that some glamorous seamstress might have acquired but they accessorize a room rather than a dress. 'I love looking at those things,' says Quartermaine, 'and I have often kept cotton spools on the mantelpiece

or in piles on books just because they are so beautiful.' It is true that when you start to look at the colours in this antique haberdashery, gleaned from trips to specialist shops in Paris, there seems no reason whatsoever why a card of ice-blue, grosgrain ribbon or a spool of gold thread should not be as ornamental, when placed on a table in a room, as they could be on the sleeve of a dress.

And when her sewing box is empty, she simply unpacks the jewellery. Of course, not everyone can boast the pair of Yves Saint Laurent earrings, that were worn by screen icon Catherine Deneuve on the cover of *Paris Match*, as the star attraction in their collection, but who wore them is only a part of their appeal. Quartermaine scatters all sorts of gems and gewgaws around. 'I have collected jars of sparkly jewellery since I was a little girl. I've still got a little plastic brooch I had when I was eight years old.' The Yves Saint Laurent earrings, used as clips on a printed tablecloth, are prized for their shape,

and against the space-age lines of the Saarinen table and stool, the collected rings, brooches and earrings look as perfect as if worn by a woman in a simple white shift.

It is clear that this artist dresses her rooms with the same insouciance as she dresses herself. It seems as natural to tie a length of ribbon around her neck and string a crystal pendant through it as to tie pretty glass shapes to a window frame where they can catch the light. 'I find a mix of glass and fabric fascinating,' she says, 'and there is something particularly mesmerizing about shot organza and prisms of light.' She is breaking boundaries again as she creates her own brand of indoor jewellery.

Quartermaine is happy to see fabrics as decorative surfaces in their own right, as opposed to merely the backdrop to everything else. This is what is so magical about her interiors. Exquisite costumes — the frou-frou skirt of a tutu or the mad extravagance of a matador's jacket — come out of the closet to be hung on walls like paintings in a gallery. This may seem surprising to traditional decorators, but it is a concept that is not so alien in Japan where kimonos are both art form and costume, appreciated for their history and the craftsmanship that goes into stitching them as well as how they make the wearer look.

So, very much in the vein of costume as ornament, an eighteenth-century gilet, with its delicate periwinkle-blue embroidery

Encrusted embroidery on an antique waistcoat finds a spontaneous reflection in costume jewellery scattered over fabrics; the falling pattern is unconsciously echoed by a pair of Yves Saint Laurent earrings.

The almost unlimited vocabulary of
Quartermaine's use of fabrics invokes an
assortment of moods and feelings — from
unashamedly frivolous frou-frous and
frills to the sober elegance of an antique
waistcoat, framed by light and displaying in its rents and marks the weight of
its history. Her use of pale colours —
lilacs, pinks and mint greens — give a
sense of softness and feminity, while contrasts of sheer and opaque are eternally
fascinating, and the interplay of light
and shade, of refraction and reflection, of
crystal and shot organza, of colour and
barely-there neutrals all highlight
the sexiness of the fabrics.

and lilac buttons, is pushed into another dimension when it is hung at a window and framed by sunshine. Looking at it close up is rather like peering at paint applied to a canvas. And although the silk has become stained and spotted through age and wear, that, too, is very beautiful. In fact, the way that the fabric has stiffened and cracked suggests that the jacket could be made out of paper. Attempts to patch, clean or mend it would break the spell. And anyway, this use of damaged fabrics has an illustrious pedigree. Madeleine Castaing, the legendary Parisian interior decorator, whose lengthy career relied on an abandoned use of luscious fabrics and exquisite ornaments, once lined a room with a water-stained bolt of silk. Although someone less self-assured would have declared the fabric spoiled, she was captivated by the exaggerated moiré effect. And John Fowler, the man whose taste characterized the quintessentially English look of decorators Colefax & Fowler, was famous for hacking into a length of expensive fabric, to fray the edge deliberately, before hanging the fabric as curtains.

Reference points for new ways to use fabrics, or for new designs, can come from anywhere. Trawling through art books, watching fashion shows or travelling — all these activities feed into ever-more-interesting ways of using textiles — and in this, Quartermaine is a virtuoso. But whereas others might be tempted to copy the past exactly, Quartermaine prefers to cut it up into a new take on modern glamour.

She achieves this modernity through deft spontaneity. 'Fabric should be hung in a natural way. I am not keen on fussily made curtains. All that bunching and tying

The chance creation of a jumble of fabrics on the artist's worktable could become the inspiration for the colour and texture of cushions and banners. Or silk scraps, tied impromptu into miniature turbans, could be used to select successful colour combinations. Thus, fabric becomes an object of sculptural beauty in itself.

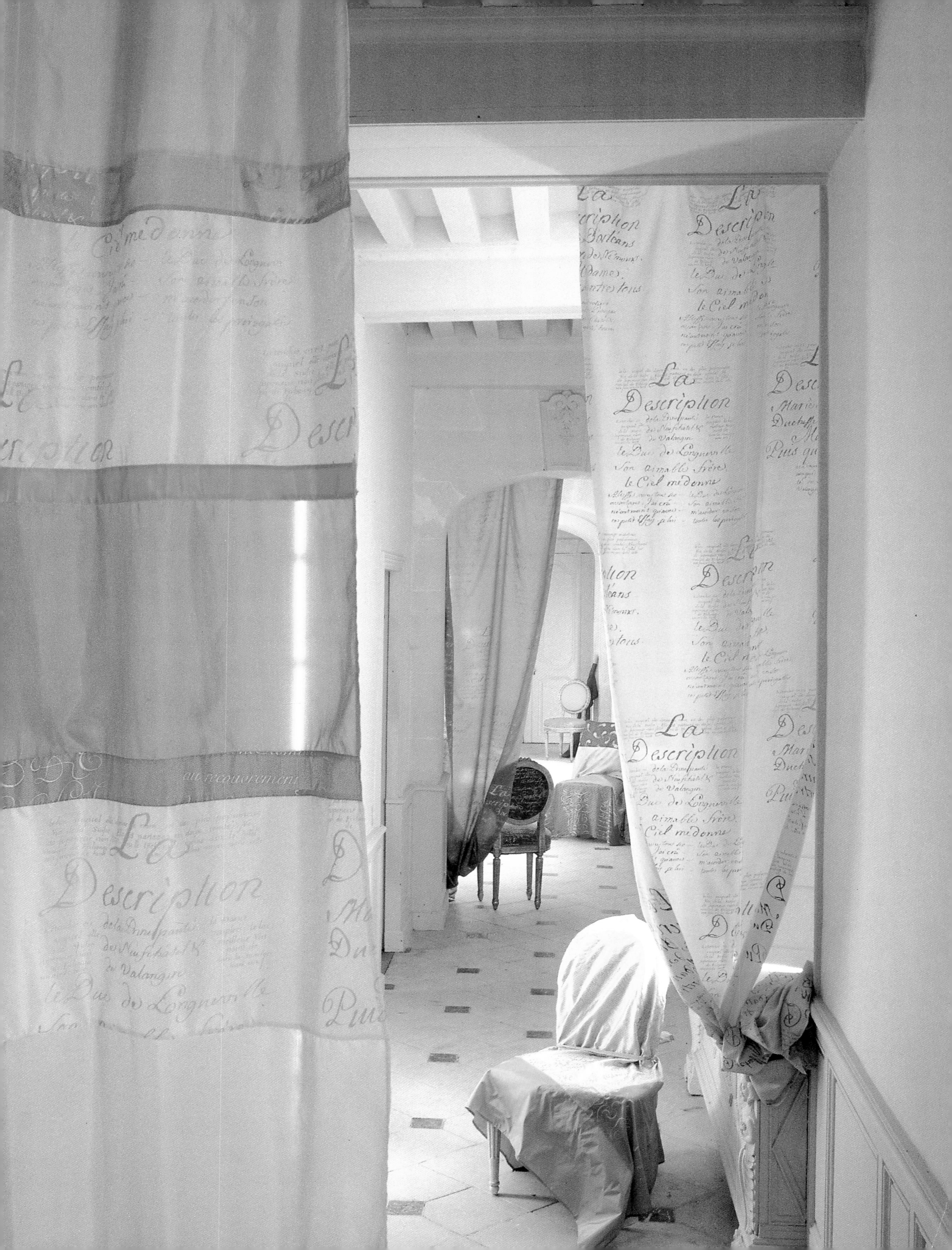
La
Description

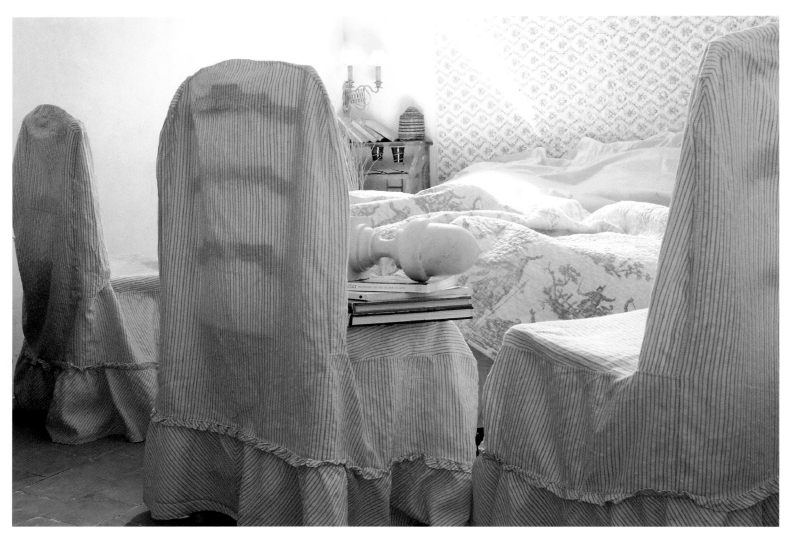

detracts from the fabric.' Instead, she prefers to hang filmy lengths of silk as banners, leaving them unlined to allow the light to pass through. And when these are hung as flat panels rather than pleated drapes, her use of colour *on* colour really can be appreciated.

The bold stripes of plain and print, cut and stitched together, were born out of a desire to have the sharpest lines possible between the colours. Dye is a notoriously wilful medium and in order to achieve, say, a line of clean pink butting up to a sharp emerald green, with maybe a thin slice of lemon in between, Quartermaine chooses to cut and reassemble, rather than print the fabric that way. It also allows her to put handpainted fabrics next to plain dyed strips or handprinted squares, mixing the different elements together as if they were a giant collage. The result is dazzling silken

flags which are as beautiful as they are versatile: they can be hung according to season or to mood, they can be used as floating doors or windows, hung as banners, or simply draped loosely over chairs.

Cushions are treated in the same way, as unique paintings which are then 'framed' or piped in contrasting colours. Although in the end the unbridled use of colour, texture and print in her selection of fabrics has an appealing air of spontaneity — almost as if a child had run riot — there is nothing haphazard in Quartermaine's artistic approach. In fact, the way each piece is planned is rigorous in the extreme. Small scraps of silk are tied into knots so that an enormous range of colour and texture can be seen at one time. Gradually, new colour combinations emerge, new relationships between texture and print

Wrapping changes familiar shapes, while allowing the inner form to be glimpsed through tantalizing layers of filmy fabric. Concealing what is normally on show and displaying what is generally hidden are recurring themes in Quartermaine's work. Previous pages: hanging fabrics on a simple rail is a sumptuous way of showing off many designs at once.

become apparent. And then everything is edited until only the most enticing remains.

The gorgeous silk-covered hangers, trailing yards of beautiful cloth, show even more graphically what the mixing colours and prints can do. The idea was inspired by a photograph of antique textiles, but as with so much of Quartermaine's approach, the original concept was refined and reworked until it became a study in colourful brio. On the end of each roll, soft-form rosettes are interspersed with feather, Persian-script or flower prints — the latter picked, perhaps, from a 1960s eiderdown or a piece of 1940s chintz — and fabric has been torn into strips for instant suspension ribbons. 'There is something tantalizing about bringing objects out into the open which are usually hidden away,' explains Quartermaine. So, on a clothes rail that others might put in a closet, she hangs her fabrics. She has even gilded it to make her point, using it like a picture rail from which to hang that day's selection of sumptuous silks.

But if there is something thrilling about revealing things that are normally concealed, there is equal excitement in wrapping up things that would typically be out on show. The idea of tying up a chandelier in a piece of cloth came from India, where lights in the temple are covered in cloth to protect them from birds. In Europe, chandeliers in châteaux and country houses were also wrapped up in dust sheets when the houses were closed up for the winter, while the furniture was dressed in loose strips of calico. In Quartermaine's modern-day version, the chandelier looks as if it has been caught, trapped almost, in a great swathe of lilac

organza. The sheerness of the wrapping and the snatches of text which you can't quite read create an air of mystery. She gives chairs and tables a similar treatment. Indeed, anything with a strong sculptural shape can look alluring when dressed in a cape of barely-there sheer. Using fabric in this way is a visual tease, a game of 'is it, or isn't it?' And it can be played anywhere. The chandelier, for example, would look as

Quartermaine expresses the sculptural potential of fabric, with visual wit. Pleated and glued silk has a look of flaking paint; satin inch-ribbons create a sense of poignant transience.

beautiful if it were done up in opaque gold organza and laid on a side table or the floor.

As in the most rarefied of Parisian *maisons des hautes coutures*, there is an emphasis on fabulous textiles in everything Quartermaine does. Seventeenth-century calligraphy, a Mozart score, poetry by Apollinaire and Braque-inspired doves all inspired one-of-a-kind textile designs for a set of French Empire chair seats, before being translated into rich furnishings and decorative ornaments. Now a fascination for words as patterning has translated to a passion for flowers, all delicately handpainted to look as if they have been cut and pressed between the pages of a book. As her work continues, they may end up mixed with stylized 1960s scrolls in a dreamy pop-art sequence.

This ability to play with fabric as a decorative surface allows for surreal effects. Lampshades look like some stylish milliner's confection, a homage to Audrey Hepburn in *Breakfast at Tiffany's*, when they are done up in Quartermaine's silk; the panels of a carved door might be used to recreate the impression of the skirt of an ancient gown, collaged with rusted, printed and artificially aged silk in true couture spirit.

It hardly comes as a surprise that new fabric designs spring from Quartermaine's own sense of style. Her passion for costume has led to impressionistic Vionnet-type flowers. It is an appealing crossover: fabrics inspired by couturiers, used to dress an interior as if it were a mannequin. Through her love affair with fabric, her instinctive use of fashion, and her absorption in the whole process of producing textiles, Quartermaine is really creating *haute couture* for the home.

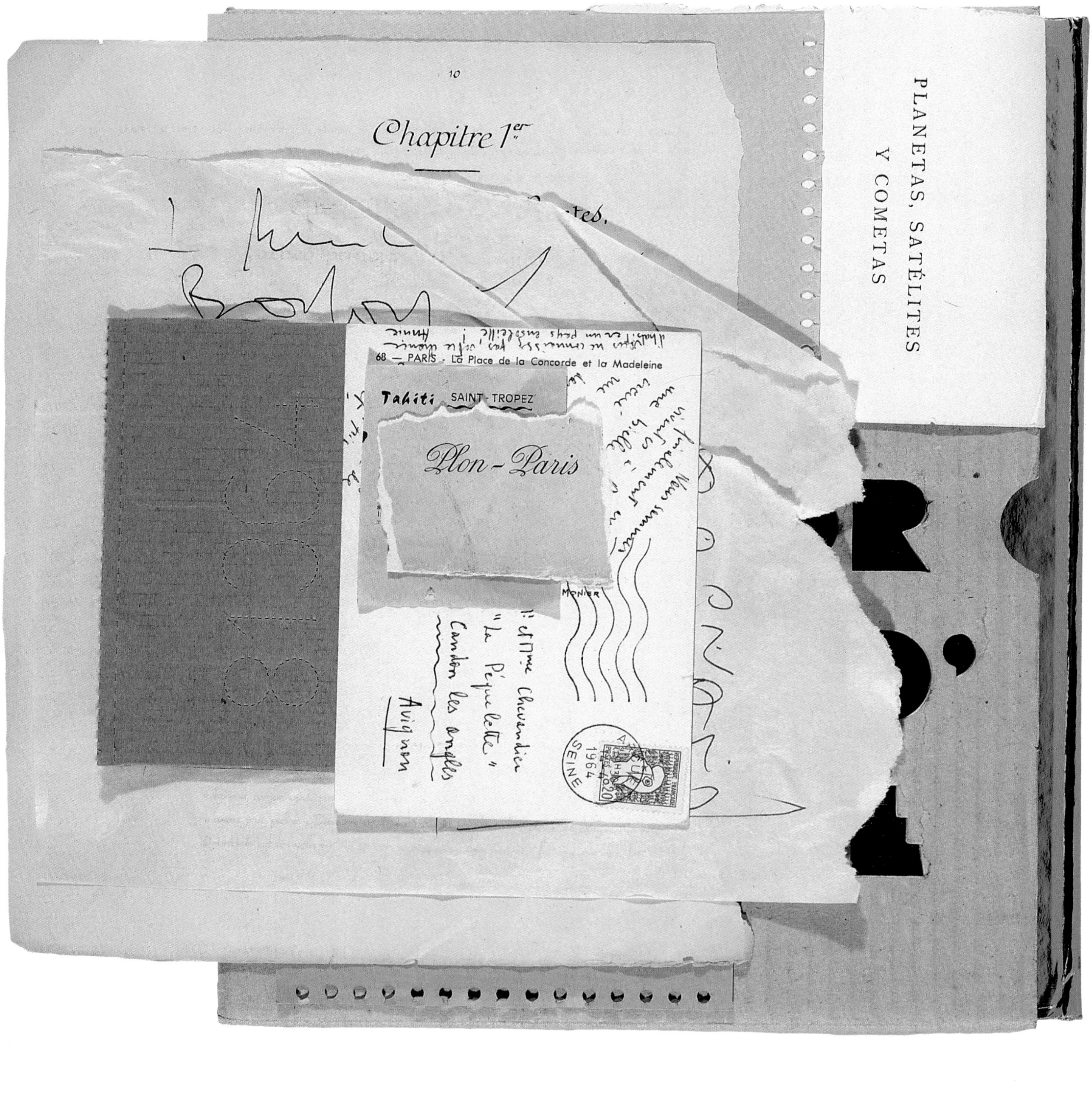
10
Chapitre 1er
PLANETAS, SATÉLITES
Y COMETAS
68 — PARIS - La Place de la Concorde et la Madeleine
Tahiti
SAINT-TROPEZ
Plon-Paris
MONIER
SEINE
1964
Avignon

Paper

'I FIRST FOUND THE BLOCKS OF *"TOILE ROYALE"* WRITING PAPER IN A DEPARTMENT STORE IN PARIS WHEN I WAS A STUDENT. AT THE TIME I COULDN'T REALLY AFFORD IT: BUYING BLOCKS OF THIS EXQUISITE PAPER JUST BECAUSE OF THAT EMBOSSED AND GILDED TOP SHEET WAS SHEER EXTRAVAGANCE. BUT I KNEW INSTANTLY — INSTINCTIVELY — THAT I HAD TO HAVE IT AND WOULD NEED IT IN A PIECE OF WORK ONE DAY.'

YEARS LATER, QUARTERMAINE IS LEFT WITH A SHELF STACKED HIGH WITH BLOCKS AND BLOCKS OF ICE-BLUE WRITING PAPER, EACH ONE STRIPPED OF THE STAMPED TOP SHEET, WHICH SHE HAS UNCEREMONIOUSLY REMOVED TO USE IN ONE OF HER MANY COLLAGES. BUT THEN, IF ANYONE IS GOING TO BE EXCITED BY THE POSSIBILITIES IN A SHEAF OF PAPER, THAT PERSON IS CAROLYN QUARTERMAINE.

In Quartermaine's vision, paper and collage — an art of layering and concealment, dextrous juxtapositions, long premeditation and swift execution — are virtually inseparable.

'Collecting paper is about collecting glimpses of history, and using it in my work brings fragments of the past into the present.'

Previous pages and above: canvases of all sizes are collaged with fine brown papers, plundered from manuscripts and notebooks, and small pieces of silk.

When it comes to paper, Quartermaine's tastes are catholic. She can be attracted to almost anything — from wispy sheets of tissue paper, which she gilds and scratches with a sharp knife to make a surface that looks like an old looking-glass, to fine brown wrapping paper, which is scored into scrolls or used in large overlapping squares like a canvas on which other papers will be positioned for one of her collages. 'I have an obsession about paper,' she acknowledges. 'I'm still sad that I could not afford a chocolate-brown box of Lalo paper when I was still studying at art college. I found it in a sale and I thought I could persuade one of the shop assistants to reduce it just a little bit more, but no.' The longing for that beautiful box of writing paper is real because this 'obsession' for paper is no mere flirtation, it is more

like a compulsion, an addiction. And it can be fuelled by any part of her life: the crinkly paper in which an amaretto biscuit is wrapped, or an envelope bearing a highly decorative foreign stamp and spidery handwriting running across its front, will be snatched up and kept for later. Similarly, pages ripped from a French chemistry book are hoarded like treasure. Even scraps of letters, torn and charred, which she found blowing in the street, were gathered up and taken home to be used and enjoyed. 'They were from the 1960s; the colour of the paper and the scrawled hand-writing were simply beautiful.' So beautiful, in fact, that a small piece of this romantic litter has been used in the corner of a deep-blue collage where it lies on a gilded fragment of fabric: the hint of a message only half-understood.

Anything can catch her eye, inflaming her passion for paper. If she is drinking coffee in a outdoor café in the heart of Milan, she may slip the printed paper napkin into her pocket; or on seeing Lanvin stockings from the 1960s, beautifully packaged with drawings by the outstanding illustrator and Dior darling René Gruau, she might have to buy the whole box.

'To me a piece of paper is as precious as a piece of silk,' she admits. And although she can afford to be more liberal in her use of the thin, brown wrapping paper she adores, than she can a costly silk, satin or velvet, expense is not really the issue. 'Pieces of paper are safeguarded just as much as a precious piece of fabric,' she says. 'And anyway, brown paper, especially when it is surrounded by gilt, can look so *luxurious*.'

But it has to be said, that in her approach to paper, Quartermaine is a little, well, promiscuous. She loves it, but she is not in awe of it. As a result, the papers she collects are thoroughly *used*. They provide the means to a very glamorous end. Just as in her other work she will take everyday items and by a clever juxtaposition, or an interesting arrangment, give them a sense of beauty that they might otherwise lack, so it is with that most simple of materials — paper. As she cuts, glues, waxes, gilds, prints, tears and scratches at the sheets, they leave behind their ordinariness, and by a process of refining and placement, are transfigured into something that is not tied to any one place or time. Simply put, these papers become art. 'I find it very difficult to think about paper without thinking about collage. With collage the end result is so much more than the sum of the parts.'

It is indeed. Quartermaine is a collage supremo, producing pieces that look at once ancient and entirely modern. And because of the diversity of the papers that she uses, and the techniques employed to make them her own, these two-dimensional, abstract works have great depth and narrative quality.

If a finished piece is any indication of what an artist is thinking, a clue to their psychological landscape, then inside Quartermaine's head everything is very stylish. There are dreams of French Empire, which are conjured up with gilded leaves and highly-stylized curlicues; there is the voice of poetry with phrases scattered like clues; there is a delicious whiff of secrecy and intrigue as semi-sheer tissues lie across half-seen words and undeciphered symbols. She plays with positive and negative, cutting out fanciful shapes like flames, scrolls or hearts and then using the paper from which the shape has been cut, like a window onto the collage beneath.

And if materials are not this beautiful to begin with, she works very hard until they are. Unlike artists who use a drift of found source material in their collages to re-define the world until it fits in with their artistic vision (think of Braque with his newsprint doves or Kurt Schwitters with his tram ticket and newspaper clippings), Quartermaine is even more radical. All the papers she uses are stamped, quite literally, with her personality. And if they are not stamped, they are printed or painted until each one is given a new surface pattern. Her methods for finding this source material can be unorthodox. 'Sometimes if I have bought an antique armchair and

Door as artist's canvas: a collage of mixed elements — gently faded, pale, scarcely-there — harmonizes subtly with the natural character of an old, lead-lined door.

In Quartermaine's work, collages capture the feeling of an antiquarian library or monastic scriptorium. The thin brown paper she loves to use has a feeling of age, and she will often pile together disparate sheets of paper until they look as if they were discovered in the corner of a study. Sheaves of paper bundled up incite the artist to delve in search of treasures — a manuscript in an anonymous spidery hand, a colour or a texture. Paper, parchment and vellum are as exquisite to her, and as mysterious and thrilling in their potential, as the most precious of fabrics.

stripped it, I will use the linen lining to mount my papers,' she explains. 'Very often it is a wonderful tea-stained colour, with perhaps the upholsterer's writing on it. If I overprint it, and then use it to back a piece of fine paper, the whole piece becomes stiff, as if it were very old.'

Papers are printed on the large worktable in her apartment. For this process, she makes up silkscreens, which are often very small, with maybe just a scrap of a design like a flower, or a line from a Keats poem. These screens are then used to handprint both paper and fabric pieces. It is a multi-faceted approach because that same line from Keats could end up on a piece of brown wrapping paper, a piece of tissue or even a sheet of cellophane. She keeps the technicalities to a minimum, using only the simplest of methods to produce the screens. 'Sometimes people can have such a complicated process for producing their work, involving expensive studios and expensive technical equipment. But you can do things very beautifully and still keep it simple.' So simple, in fact, that the method she uses to produce her screens has since been developed for use in schools.

Producing this stockpile of bespoke papers is a lengthy process, one that is never really finished. A clear plastic box is stuffed full of them, some of which could be fifteen years old, while others might have been put there yesterday. When it is time to collage, out comes the box, the papers are unpacked and the act of sifting, of playing with and placing those papers, begins. And because each piece of paper, large or small, is unique, the collage itself

is too, resisting attempts to formulate or copy. This is because collage relies on a delicate balancing act — colour versus texture, shape versus surface decoration — so that even Quartermaine is unable to recreate a successful collage the second-time around.

Getting that balance right means paring everything down, and then rejecting more; rigorously removing elements, designs, shapes or textures which she feels have no place in the finished piece. 'I edit that box all the time. Sometimes it is extremely sad to throw things away, but you instinctively know when you no

longer want certain elements in your work, and I think you have to clear them away to make more space for new thoughts and inspiration.' But editing can be a creative process too. 'There is always that moment when you open the box and start to sort through. Papers will fall out next to other papers in surprising new combinations.'

But whereas the build-up to producing a collage might take several weeks, the time taken in making a collage is much shorter. 'I love collage because it is a very instant and personal process. It either works or it doesn't.' Quite simply, she adores the

immediacy and spontaneity of this art form, and the play of materials which in themselves are so exciting.

It might seem strange, given that she has such a love of the medium, but what Quartermaine really loves is not stiff, thick, expensive paper, but the cheaper, flimsier sort. Especially prized is the brown paper that art movers use to wrap paintings and objects. On moving day it is as thick as an eiderdown, but in her hands it is pulled apart for the brown topsheet, which is so incredibly fine and translucent it could almost be mistaken for a honey-coloured silk. (Her friends even save the wrapping paper for her when they move house.) All the inexpensive papers she likes share the same quality — they are all exquisitely thin and delicate, like fabrics. Brown packing paper works well when glued to silk because the silk becomes transparent and the fine grain of the paper shows through, helping to 'fix' all the elements in a collage and give it a sense of structure. It is a visual device similar to the heavy creases in a pure white tablecloth over which flowers have been carelessly scattered; it acts as a grid for chance encounters of a kind, and brings unity to apparently random individual elements.

Parchment is also a favourite because of its deep creamy colour and its texture. Pages from old books, which have yellowed with age around the edges and become torn or fingered, are also on her shortlist

of favourite materials. Old legal documents were fished out of a skip in south-east London and taken home to flesh out her collection of old papers. 'I just couldn't leave them there,' she laughs. 'They were all land registry documents from way back when, all beautifully handwritten. Sometimes I am tormented by the fact that I didn't manage to retrieve more of them.' Even old newspapers might catch her attention — not because of the headlines but because of the way the newsprint has aged, turning a lustrous golden, browny yellow.

And if she knows what she likes, then equally she knows what she doesn't like. She prefers not to use Japanese papers, which have their own pattern and texture — with rare exceptions. 'I did once use a very small scrap of Japanese paper, postcard size,' she admits, 'because it was so thick I could almost embed the print marks into it.' Equally, anything with a pressed flower in it is outlawed.

Paper is not used simply to make up two-dimensional collages. Sometimes Quartermaine will dispense altogether with the backing to her work and apply her papers and fabrics straight onto walls, doors or objects. The lead-lined door in the bedroom of a French château was the perfect candidate for this treatment. The strip of silver metal acted like a frame, with tacks still holding small threads of the fabric that had been used to cover the door previously. And somehow, when the collage had been completed, the door looked even more ancient. Quartermaine's collages might camouflage the original object, but in doing so they also seem to reveal and accentuate the inherent character and texture of a surface.

She has also collaged straight onto walls, treating the whole expanse as one giant canvas for self-expression. When her use of collage is this liberated, the delicate balance between walls, floor and furniture is heightened considerably. For example, if the floors are polished concrete or simple tiles, then the ideal place for the collage would be walls, with the furniture and furnishings kept very low-key; perhaps just plain white sofas. But if she were to collage the chair backs or other pieces of furniture, then she would want to balance that with plain white walls. 'It is about knowing when and where to stop,' she explains. 'About knowing where you want the eye to rest.'

Previous pages: wrappers from sugar cubes or Italian biscotti, lining paper from a drawer will all find their way into her paper box to be over printed or painted, to take on another life.

This idea of applying collage to objects and surfaces first started back at college when she began painting straight onto ceramic pots. She would select particular shapes and have the pots specially thrown. Her enthusiasm for this led to further experimentation with collage on papier-mâché — plates and cones — and, later, onto large hardboard screens.

Why plates? 'It is simply that I have always loved and collected antique plates and it was a new shape to work on.' And so she kept this circular form in the papier-mâché plates she had made up, and glamorized them with exquisite gilding and delicious lines of text.

And cones? She would collage them and place them on mantelpieces, in fireplaces, or on gilded stands, where they stood like relics from the wardrobe of some beautifully dressed wizard. This is a shape she adores for its associations with theatricality and magic.

The screens come from her love of decorative surfaces that are not too fixed. Her taste is for anything that can be moved, folded or used in another setting because it adds to the feeling of spontaneity and fluidity that all her interiors share. It is as if a collage were applied to a wall, but a wall that can walk.

And there is a sense of motion in her work; a sense that all the elements have somehow been caught and trapped like butterflies; a sense that a solid surface has

been made more ethereal, less substantial, merely by the layers of papers which she has so delicately applied. This is accentuated on a screen on which a sheet of printed, semi-transparent tissue paper has been glued. The design was taken from a set of travel books from the 1940s, illustrated by Jean Cocteau, with the addition of a word from the cover of an Italian notebook which caught Quartermaine's eye. It is characteristic of the way she works — an element picked up here, a line picked up there, mixed together until she creates something which embodies visually the line on the bottom of an expensive bottle of perfume, 'London, Paris, New York'. The scratches of gilt on a whisper of a printed paper heart give the impression of antique glass, while a fine ornamental metal chair, weighted down with nothing more than a loose roll of paper, underlines the delicacy of her work.

She uses paper to transform and translate — and maybe that is why the antique

papier-mâché drops sent from Milan by a friend so attracted her. These are pretty, delicate objects which, quite simply, are paper translated into something else. Now they have been transformed into beads on a curtain, standing in for more orthodox fringing. Quartermaine also translates paper into other media, using paper shredders, for example, to turn copies of comic books into exotic raffia. 'These comics have a particular three-colour printing process,' she explains. 'And when the pages are shredded, you are left with these incredibly fine multicoloured strips which can then be glued flat until they look like crazy African mats.'

However, this love of paper is not just about creating art, nor is it about an ability to create luxurious objects out of simple everyday things, or to add a lick of glamour to a furl of yesterday's *Financial Times*, even a pile of receipts and bills; this passion is more intrinsically a part of Quartermaine's everyday life. For example, flowers given to a friend will always be wrapped appealingly; presents, too. 'I can spend hours cutting paper into tassels to ensure that something is beautifully wrapped. It becomes part of the present, part of the experience. The only problem is that having taken the trouble to wrap flowers in beautiful paper, and maybe tie them with a ribbon, you then see that paper discarded. To me the paper is just as beautiful as anything else.'

Above: more favourite things. Italian papier-mâché beads are sewn onto the fringe of a silk curtain. Inscribed tissue paper and monoprinted birds add to the impression of fragility.

Layers of 'dirty ecru' sugar papers are built up with glue, and further fragments — book covers, inscribed tissue paper, handprinted strips — are carefully interleaved on top, with a final layer of water-based glue acting as a glaze. The resulting effect is typical of Quartermaine's style: subtle, elusive, fragile and suggestive. This same technique is applied with equal assurance to a miscellany of different objects, ranging from wall surfaces, folding screens and chair backs to a papier-mâché vase and plates.

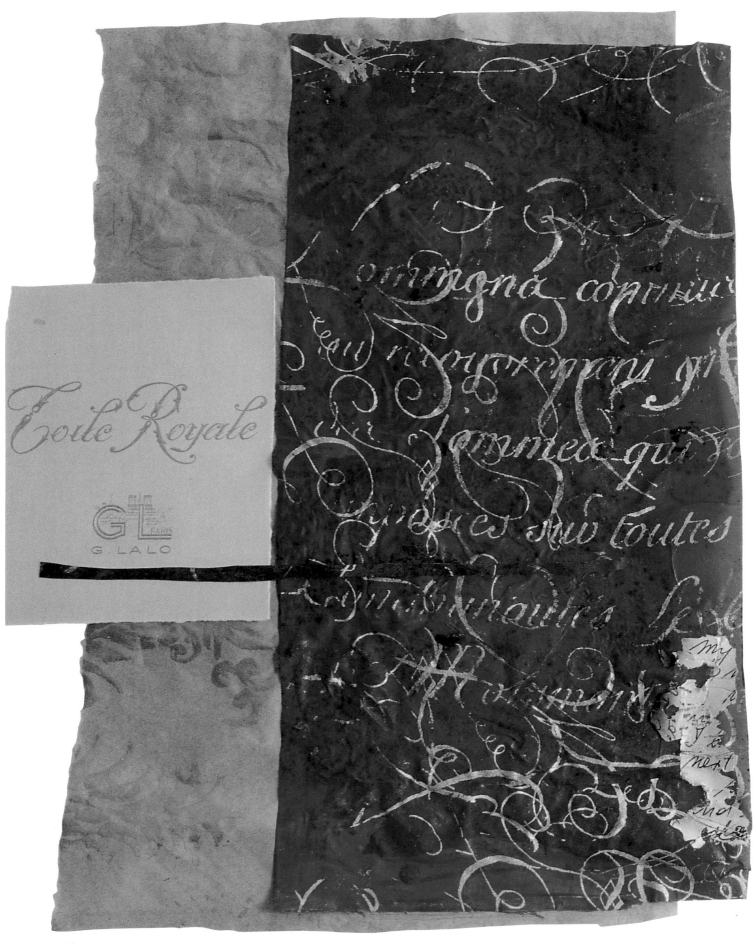

A diptych exploring and exploiting the possibilities of mark-making and scratch-making, and the contrast (a joy to Quartermaine) between the imprinting of the silk-screen

*process and the embossing of the Toile Royale cover paper. A torn fragment of a
burned letter punctuates the hectic jumble of overprinting.*

I was due back after one month in Egypt but I've torn up my return ticket & scattered the paper

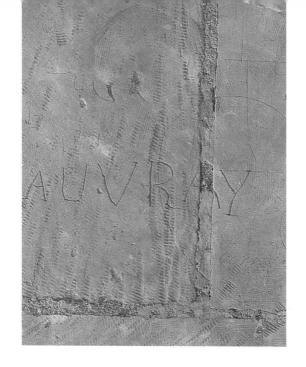

Paint

'WHATEVER ELSE I DO IN MY LIFE, I KNOW THAT THE FEELING I HAVE FOR PAINT IS SO STRONG THAT IT IS UNLIKELY TO GO AWAY. I HAVE THIS IMMEDIATE RESPONSE WHEN I SEE A BAG OF PIGMENT OR A JAR OF LIQUID COLOUR. IN FACT, MY RESPONSE IS SO POWERFUL THAT EVEN WALKING INTO A STUDIO CAN SET ME THINKING. IT MUST BE SOMETHING TO DO WITH THAT PARTICULAR SMELL OF THE OIL PAINT AND THE TURPENTINE. IT IS SUCH A MAGIC FEELING TO BE SURROUNDED BY THOSE MATERIALS.

'AND THEN I ALWAYS GET A REAL THRILL WHEN I FIRST PUT MY BRUSH INTO THE LIQUID AND BEGIN TO PAINT. THE PROCESS IS SO WONDERFUL THAT THE ACTUAL RESULT SEEMS OF LITTLE OR NO IMPORTANCE COMPARED TO THE ACT OF LOADING THE BRUSH WITH PAINT AND MOVING IT ACROSS THE PAPER OR FABRIC. PAINT IS SO MUCH ABOUT POSSIBILITY, ABOUT CREATED WORLDS, ABOUT LAYERING, TEXTURE AND SURFACE. BUT MOSTLY IT IS ABOUT THAT PHYSICAL PROCESS OF DIPPING YOUR BRUSH, OR MAYBE JUST YOUR HANDS, INTO THIS POOL OF WET, DRIPPING COLOUR.'

For Quartermaine paint is colour, intoxicating in its
depths, its lush beauty, its raw energy, its extreme delicacy
and the power of its emotional reverberations.

Intense colour, dense and saturated or glowing and luminescent, is the essence of paint for Quartermaine. Opposite: pure pigment presents paint in its rawest state; canvases by Mark Rothko (such as "Untitled", 1960) show pigment at its most transcendent.

Carolyn Quartermaine is fascinated by paint; by the way it looks (when graffiti is scratched into a painted wall), by the way it behaves (sinking into paper, bleeding into other colours), and by what artists choose to do with it. 'Take Bonnard, for instance. He used to hang lots of his canvases, his work in progress, along the length of a wall and apply dots of colour — first to this painting, then to that. He worked on many canvases at a time, creating wonderful, living colours with paint.'

When you enter the world of an artist, you enter a world driven by vision, inspiration and imagination, but it is a world that can only be unlocked and communicated by an artistic process, a technique of using materials to pin down and express emotion. Through the methods they choose, artists turn what they feel into things that we can see. Of course, the materials they choose are varied, but what they are most often seduced by is — paint. Maybe it is something to do with the potential in taking a material that is dry, turning it into a liquid, and using it to fix an emotion by applying it to canvas, and then letting it dry once again.

'When I look at a Rothko canvas, I am drawn into the way that he uses paint,' confesses Quartermaine. 'The canvases glow, they are quiet and deep, and the colours look as if they are floating on the wall. To me, those paintings have a spirituality and a moodiness about them that is very special.' She cites Craigie Aitchison as another artist whose use of paint is inspiring because of the way he seems to have trapped particles of light in the pigment to produce works of strange luminosity. 'What I love is the way those artists retain the quality of the paint they are using,' she says. 'It gives me a sense of freedom to look into a canvas so saturated with colour, so intense that it seems to pulsate.'

What she also loves about paint is its potential for creating texture, both the visual impression and the physical reality of it. She recalls the excitement of seeing the work of Gillian Ayres at the Royal Academy in London. 'I was bowled over by the physicality of her paint. It looks as if it has just been flicked over with a palette knife, and is about an inch thick on

ARTICLES de PARIS
PARFUMERIE
TISSUS
SE
NSE
AFM
France 3
EU
Grand

the canvas. There is such texture to it; it is so rich. Paint used like this is very sexy. You really want to get up close to it. And when you add this to an inspired use of colour . . .'

Her assessment of Ayres's art partly explains her own fascination for paint. For her, paint is very much to do with texture and it is very much to do with colour — or rather about recreating colour, intensifying colour, manipulating colour.

And so her own reputation as an inspired colourist comes not just from an emotional response to the world around her but from her working relationship with paint. It is a relationship that has evolved over the years through her training as an artist to the point where she began applying paint not just to canvas, as the fine art diktat demands, but to fabric, walls and furniture. Although she now uses paint in an entirely personal way, her years at art school have given her a solid foundation and her singular use of paint is backed by an in-depth knowledge of fine art and its history — not only of the way artists use paint to achieve their

Peeling signwriting on weathered Mediterranean walls.
Quartermaine's own photographs testify to her
enduring fascination with the infinite variations
in style and lettering, the effects of texture and the
resonance of history, in all their faded, multilayered glory.

own particular slice of reality, but also of a battery of fine art techniques from how to prepare a canvas, to mixing oils and glazes, to working with watercolours and pigments. In other words, she took time to learn all the rules before deciding which ones to break.

Painting is a physical process, a way of getting from the imaginary 'here' inside your head, to the concrete 'there' of a finished piece of fabric, collage or painting. It is a way of transferring colour from tube, can or bag to wall, fabric or canvas. Not much is lost in the translation. 'When I look into a bag of pure pigment,' Quartermaine says, 'I get a rush of excitement at the intensity of this beautiful colour.' For her, the best painted surfaces are those that preserve that sense of the possibility of paint in its rawest, purest form.

She adores Bonnard, whose canvases are so luminescent that it is as if the paint acts as a prism, splitting everything into pools of coloured light. 'He was an exact, figurative painter,' she explains, 'but he was painting so much more than you could ever see. Everything is charged with this inner vibrancy; even his whites contain colour.'

She constantly uses cultural pointers to explain particular effects that she admires, or is trying to achieve. For example, she will mention Anish Kapoor or Yves Klein to illustrate a point about how pure pigment can capture a mood, and then quickly move on to illustrate a point with reference to Picasso before recalling a show of Jennifer Durrant's in the Museum of Modern Art in Oxford, England. 'There were four enormous canvases which had been covered in

Old walls, mottled and flaking, scuffed and streaked, offer as much pleasure and inspiration to Quartermaine as fine paintings. Present her with a blank wall and she will paint it into the advanced stages of decay.

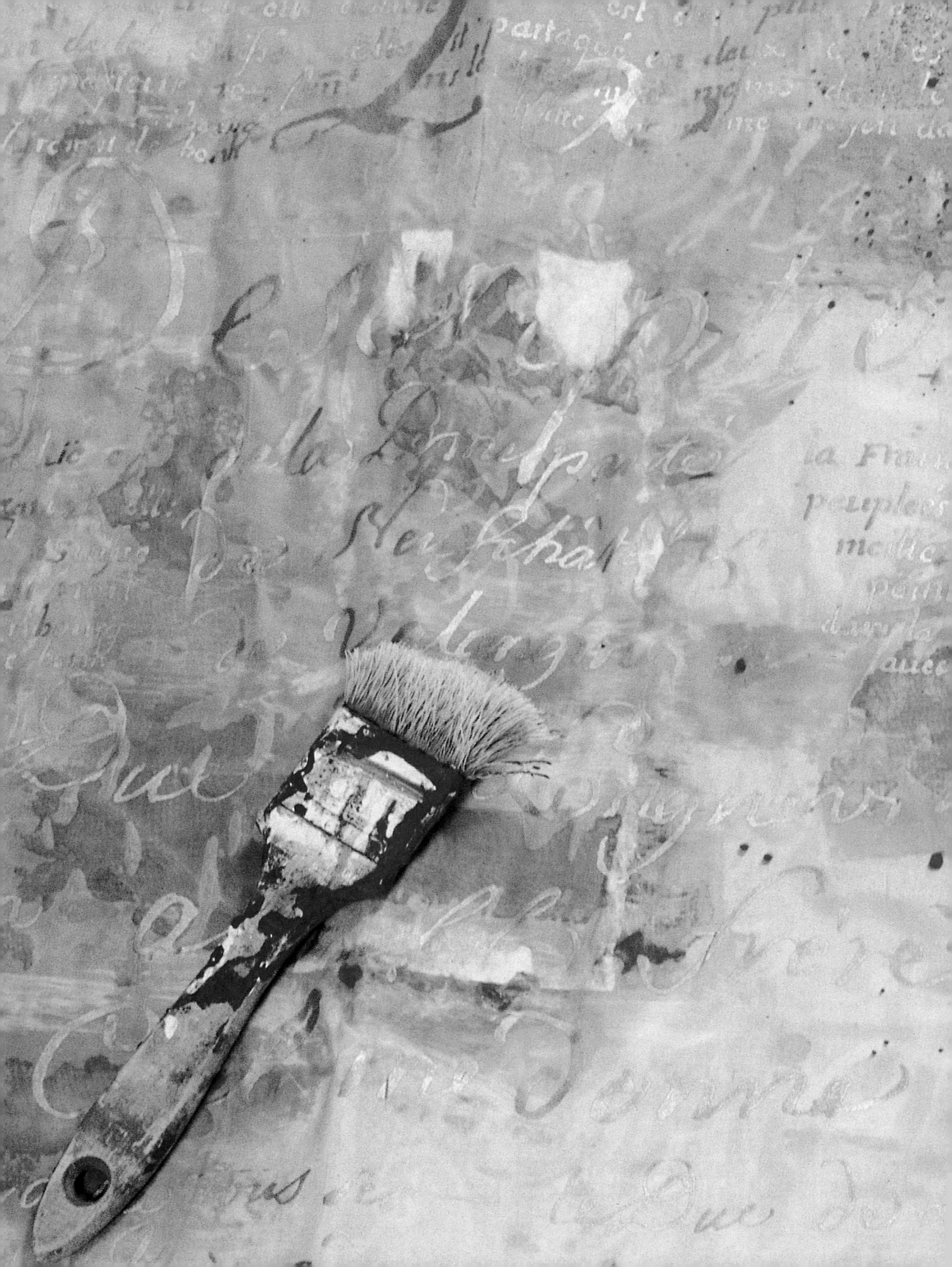

delicate washes of colour to which huge monoprinted leaf shapes had been added, the edges highlighted in glitter.' About the same time, she came across the work of the American pattern painters, among them Robert Kushner and Kim MacConnel who showed their work at the Holly Solomon Gallery in New York in the late 1970s and later in Cork Street, London. 'It was wild work,' she says, 'inspired by the textile designs and American kitsch of the 1950s. These artists painted strips of fabric with bold graphics: planes, stars, moons, you name it.' And then they went one stage further, applying yet more to the surface to make the whole thing even richer. 'It seemed new and fresh and, dare I say it, decorative,' she says. 'In the fine art world, there is quite a prejudice against the decorative or applied

arts. Unless you are applying your paint onto a canvas, your work is not deemed to be serious enough. But here was this highly decorative work being shown in the heart of the modern art establishment. I loved the fact that fine art could also be decorative.'

But what draws her to paint — and keeps her fascination — could just as easily be the peeling, flaking wall of a building in Rome or Florence, walls where the heat and the sun has cracked the layers of distemper until it flakes away in uneven patches to reveal the stone beneath. 'A good wall has the same spellbinding quality as a Twombly or a Rothko painting for me,' says Quartermaine. 'I love the mottled marks, the mould, the flaking caused by pollution, the scratch marks of the graffiti.' In a very

Depths of blue-dyed fabric against delicate washes of blue on Quartermaine's studio wall reveal the potential for the variety of feeling in different intensities of colour. Previous pages: In this collage, Quartermaine poured blue paint onto white silk and allowed it to collect in deep pools before rubbing in some blue powder pigment.

real way, what excites her about these walls is the same thing that she is trying to create in her own collages. 'I am drawn to a feeling of time passing,' she says, 'of that feeling that paint has been built up over the years and then has been worn away again, either by chance, or by the weather, or by intent. What is revealed underneath the paint is as interesting as the texture of the paint that is left behind. I photograph walls like that endlessly. In fact, walking around Rome, I sometimes feel that I want to take the walls home and hang them in my apartment like paintings.'

If she gets pleasure from looking at these surfaces, the flick of recognition as they connect with ideas and pictures inside her head, then the real fun starts when the paints come out. And, as one might expect by looking at her work, she is anything but purist in her approach. If she manages to achieve effects of exquisite delicacy and beauty, it is not without getting her hands just a little dirty. Painting, Quartermaine-style, is a very physical process. She might mix up huge jars of pigments, paints and dyes to paint panels of silk for a collage; she might even move her table outside into the garden so that the paint will dry faster; and then, using a mix of paints — acrylics, watercolours, oils and dyes — she might set about pouring paint in great lush pools onto the silk. 'It is as much a passion for the physicality of pouring paint,' she says 'and building up colour, as for anything else.'

Quartermaine might feel a green mood coming on, brought about by looking at a length of her own wonderful pistachio silk. And when it does, she will set out her

paints and work at mixing up different shades of green in anything from an aqueous wash of eau-de-Nil household emulsion to the sharpest, most intense emerald gouache. Then she will pour the emulsion onto the silk, either using her hands to sweep the liquid colour backwards and forwards across the fabric, or else moving the colour until it lies in deep pools here, or a semi-transparent sheen there, with great, soft, wide brushstrokes. Where the paint is at its thickest, soaking through the silk, this is where it will dry stiff and crackled as a piece of paper. At its thinnest, it will look like a soft, semi-sheer fabric. 'And then I might have a cobalt-blue day,' she laughs. 'It all depends on how I am feeling.'

For her, the thrill comes in trying to control the uncontrollable. All these paints behave differently. They are mixed in different strengths, they run across the fabric, soak into watery blotches, or stay exactly where they are, in definite marks. 'It is so exciting to have these jars and tubes of fabulous, intense colour around

you,' explains Quartermaine. 'But what comes out of those jars of orange or blue or green is even more magical. The way the colours seep into each other, bleed into each other, is stunning. And you are always there watching, watching all the time, trying to control the wash of colour.'

The choice of paint depends on what she is trying to achieve. 'Household emulsion,' she muses. 'Now that is about big space, big quantities, whereas gouache, those tiny tubes, is about more intense, delicate mark-making.' Then there are the acrylic paints to be mixed in with powders until she has large buckets of colour. 'And I do like to use specialist textile dyes. They can be combined with a binder or mixed in with an emulsion paint. The colour is so strong,' she enthuses, 'that you could re-colour an entire continent with a drop.' She will also use these dyes with water rather than the prescribed binder so that she can pour and spatter and splash them onto her chosen fabric. 'Yes, it is very messy,' she concedes. 'You do have to

know that you can drip and drop and pour without worrying about making a mess on the floor.'

She has favourite brushes, favourite tricks of her extremely decorative trade. There are wonderfully soft, wide brushes to sweep paint across large expanses of coloured silk, or else to dust pigment powders onto paint already semi-dry. And then there are stiffer, harder, older brushes for the more definite mark-making, which might come after she has built up those layers of semi-transparent washes. 'I might take a blue silk and mix up an indigo or purple emulsion and pour it into the silk to make the colour more intense,' she explains. 'But that colour would float unless something pinned it down, such as the merest lick of colour flicked on with a fine brush, or a different shape printed, painted or stamped on top.' Once she has mixed and poured, she will add oil paints, or rub in powder pigment, or indeed do anything she fancies before letting the fabric dry completely. And even that may not be the end. She

may decide to overprint the fabric, or glue the silk to huge, rusted, aged and decaying metal sheets. When the glue has dried, the silk is ripped away from the metal to leave panels of coppery-coloured rust, stamped onto the fabric which the glue has stiffened. 'The fabric looks like paper, and if you touch it it crackles and crunches.' Over the years the metal sheets start to look like canvases themselves; something of the design on the fabric and of the paint gets left behind, and these layers build up over time. 'I keep them outside to rust them even more, and then when they look really patinated I bring them in and prop them up on the mantelpiece,' she explains.

'Helen Frankenthaler is an artist whose work I admire very much,' Quartermaine says. 'I sense a rapport between what I am trying to express and what she has achieved. With paint, it is all about controlling accidents, knowing when to pull back and when to let the paint do what it wants to do.' Quartermaine is thinking of a series of huge monoprints

which Frankenthaler did in the 1960s. The process she used required the transfer of the design onto a large flat stone, and the application of ink or paint before pressing the stone down onto a sheet of paper. Because of the differences in the amount of colour applied in the first place, and the way the paint or ink was pushed into the paper, each of the prints is slightly different. Frankenthaler's prints have that wonderful quality that can be created by over-printing and painting.

'I love to print,' admits Quartermaine, 'but I love to use my hands, too. There is such a primitive pleasure when you push paint around with your fingers or the heel of your palm. And if you use this method, then, like Frankenthaler, you can experience how the liquid paint acts without any interference, how it stains, runs and bleeds, whilst trying to control the process so that you ultimately end up with something beautiful.'

Her absorption in this process is shown by an attachment to her tools and raw materials. 'Over the years, the jars in which

Over the years, artists' materials and tools develop their own beauty. The thick texture of gold textile paint looks almost edible, like honey; collected on the hairs of a sable brush it becomes like strands of gold embroidery thread; and the build-up of paint on the handle creates an exquisite patina as it wears away over time.

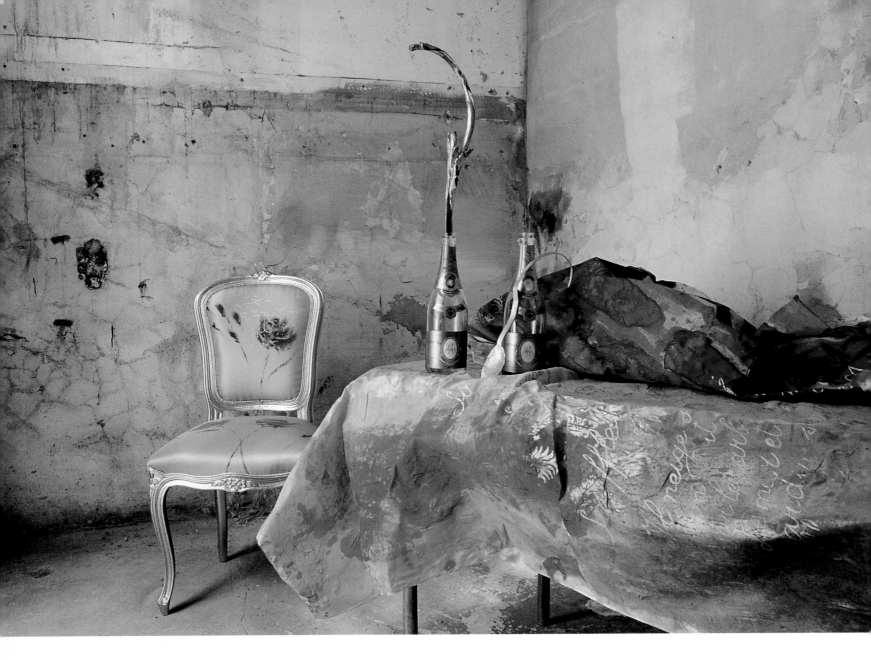

I mix the paints have developed into something special in their own right.' And certainly, looking at the mix of jars and buckets, and palettes dressed in rainbow colours, or brushes turned to gold through repeated application of the soft gold paint that she adores, you see that she is right. 'The tools of your trade become beautiful objects,' she says. 'I sometimes think that looking at an artist's palette can be as appealing as looking at the finished canvas.'

The way she employs different techniques and paints on the same piece of fabric is what gives her work such resonance. And it is always rooted in her appreciation of fine art. 'Miró's paintings really inspired me to experiment with dropping paint onto wet fabric,' she says. 'The silk has to be really sopping so that

the colour will bleed out. But you also have to be very disciplined about how much paint you drop down. In my flower prints, for example, the paint has to flow out so that it looks like the petals of a flower, but not so much that it looks like a messy mark.' This is where you need to exercise control over the paint. 'I love the watercolour effect that it creates.' Her ability to be both entirely free with her paints and extremely disciplined means that those free Miróesque washes are subsequently 'fixed' by fine flicks of black ink, and 'framed' by the gilt of a chair back.

If she likes to play with paint on fabric, she is equally willing to play with it on other surfaces. And when she applies her couture approach to paint on a surface that is already marked or distressed in

some way — a wall, say — the effect can be to further age and romanticize that surface. Left alone with a blank wall, she will spend the same amount of time as another artist might take over a canvas. She is happy to spend hours with coloured washes, building up layers of watery colour onto the haphazard marks already on a wall. When she diluted emerald green household emulsion until it looked more like tinted water, and then applied this onto a cellar wall in great uneven strokes, it had the strange effect of not only exaggerating the defects of the wall, but also of lifting the whole scene into something more romantic and historical.

'There is something very special about a length of wonderful fabric or an exquisite gilded chair against an uneven, pitted wall,' she explains. 'I love the contrast of

Quartermaine uses paint to create a romantic vision of history and the antique. Here she covered a heavily marked wall with washes in shades of green, allowing them to seep into the cracks and so accentuate the surface texture. Then she took lengths of silk and poured layer upon layer of lime, emerald and aquamarine dye onto them, creating deep lakes of green (like Lake Como, she explains). After rusting and over-printing it, she then played with the contrasts by juxtaposing it with a chair upholstered in dyed silk of pristine purity.

textures and colours. That is what paint is really about.' To illustrate this further, she points to the work of David Seidner, the American fashion photographer whose work she much admires. What Seidner has managed to achieve in his photographic compositions is a feeling of extraordinary texture as well as depth. Paloma Picasso's face stares into the camera, shattered into shards in a modern reworking of one of her father's cubist portraits. In fact, her face seems to be reflected in ripples on a black lake. In another picture, a model appears through a glass pane, just enough of the smudged glass wiped clean to reveal her face and torso.

And then there are the pictures of eighteenth- and nineteenth-century costumes, which she immediately fell in love with when she saw them on a street in Paris, posters for the Musée de la Mode. The clothes were modelled on elegant wicker mannequins, and had been photographed against a concrete wall that looked like a bare cell. The effect was dramatic, with the unsophisticated wicker mannequins throwing the gorgeously embroidered fabric of the gowns into even sharper relief. 'I loved those pictures,' remembers Quartermaine. 'I ran straight to the museum and bought a set of postcards which I kept in my studio for a long time. There was a feeling in them that I found immensely inspiring; some images are so in tune with what the originator is trying to communicate that it is almost as if you have seen them somewhere before. That is exactly what I felt about those postcards.'

'L'estel Matinal' by Joan Miró, 1946. Miró's paintings inspired Quartermaine to drop watered-down textile paint onto silk to represent flowers, going over them lightly with a few lines of ink to suggest their stems.
Overleaf: Quartermaine's handpainting technique uses loose, vigorous, quick strokes for the full blooms of the flowers.

Food

'I HAVE THIS MEMORY OF A WONDERFUL MEAL. I WENT TO ROME TO VISIT FRIENDS AND WE STAYED IN PRINCE DORIA PAMPHILLI'S PALAZZO. IT WAS AUGUST AND WE DECIDED TO HOLD A DINNER PARTY IN THE FORMAL DINING ROOM. I REMEMBER THAT IT HAD AN AMAZING CEILING AND A PAIR OF CANDELABRA ON THE TABLE THAT WERE SO HEAVY THEY COULD HAVE KILLED SOMEONE.

'ON THE DAY OF THE PARTY, WE WERE LATE COMING BACK FROM THE BEACH. FIFTEEN OR TWENTY GUESTS WERE INVITED, SO I QUICKLY TOOK SOME NEWSPAPER AND LAID IT OUT ON THE DINING TABLE INSTEAD OF A CLOTH . . . THEN I FOUND THESE HUGE BRANCHES AND PLACED THEM DOWN THE CENTRE OF THE TABLE. THESE OPPOS-ING ELEMENTS — THE ROUGHNESS OF THE NEWSPAPER AND THE GNARLED BRANCHES — LOOKED STUNNING IN THAT BEAUTIFUL ROOM. I DON'T REMEMBER WHAT WE ATE.'

*Food as spectacle, fantasy and art form: deftly arranged
in visual conceits and mouthwatering plays of colour and
texture, Quartermaine's culinary creations are a feast
for the imagination.*

'There are many surreal possibilities in the juxtaposition of fruit, confectionary and other foods with favourite commonplace objects.'

Tableaux of texture and contrast play on the perennial Quartermaine themes of layering and wrapping. Plump pears are cradled in a sugar basket. Miniature still-lifes of frosted fruit are held in cake rings. Overleaf: Simple apples and pears are wrapped in mantles of antique paper.

Like so much of Quartermaine's work, indeed like so much of her life, this dinner — conjured out of nowhere on a hot evening in Rome — has an extraordinary cinematic quality about it. Beautiful rooms, candlelight, a sumptuously set table, the guests about to arrive — the whole scene is so charged with atmosphere that it could be a scene from an Italian art-house movie. This is food as theatre, as ceremony, as a dramatic experience. And while not everyone gets to borrow the sumptuous backdrop of a palazzo in which to eat dinner and entertain their friends, still there is an attitude in the way both the food and the table are prepared — spontaneously, and yet with a real sense of the theatricality of dining, which owes very little to glamorous surroundings or to sumptuous menu. It comes from a way of seeing, an approach that treats the whole experience as a gloriously decadent picnic. There can be little doubt that had the room been a small, undistinguished white box, Quartermaine would have somehow managed to create an equally memorable atmosphere.

You get the impression that when Quartermaine prepares dinner, the most important ingredient is fantasy. She loves to indulge in the alchemy that transforms a measure or two of granulated sugar into a delicate, gold-coloured, finely woven basket for poached pears, or that whisks egg whites into the palest of meringues before piling them up in a towering cone, like a pearl-studded sorcerer's hat.

While Quartermaine's presentation of food looks ornate, delicate and romantic, much of it is actually very simple. While

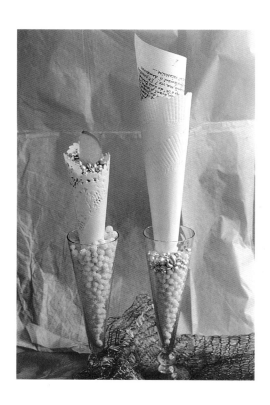

she likes the food she prepares to look beautiful, she is not into foodie-style fuss. Arrangements take her only moments to assemble, using elements culled from her pantry, her worktable, her studio. And this is what makes the food so alluring — and so unexpected. Different moods will dictate alternative and unusual serving suggestions and settings. She could just as easily serve elegant ratafia biscuits in a cellophane bag (the cellophane hand-printed by her, of course) as put them on a plate. She is just as likely to drink *caffé latte* out of pretty Turkish glasses because she likes the colour of the milky coffee next to the gilding on the glass, or hand around *calisson* sweets, those thick almond-paste confections covered with an even thicker layer of white icing, straight from their cardboard box, as bother with the fuss

Let them eat pink! Display, colour and daring are of the essence. Quartermaine enjoys using garish, edible colours — opposing natural and synthetic greens, pinks and yellows — and creating surreal compositions such as limes on chairs and edible letters.

of a *brûlée* or a *soufflé*. Flying in the face of foodie convention — diktats that say that china should be simple and white, so that nothing detracts from the focus on food — at a Quartermaine feast it is very unlikely that the plates will be white. In fact, there may not be a plate in sight at all. This is because the food is only one part of her overall scheme, the edible part in an arrangement that more often looks like a composition for a still-life or a photograph. Quite simply, she treats food in the same way that she does a pile of silks and papers out of which a collage will be created.

'Food presentation is to do with the choice of a few carefully selected elements,' explains Quartermaine. 'I think of it as a very personal process. Yes, it is artistic, but not in any overworked sense. My approach is very "of the moment".' Indeed, placing sugar-dusted fruit pastries on the pale cover of a book is a deliciously modern and unexpected reworking of the act of taking tea on a fine china tea plate.

Quartermaine enjoys the scale of this composition, arrested in time like a chess game, with pieces made from flowers set in pastel-coloured ice. Her favourite lilac shade is the dominant note, the suave printed silk contrasting with the grainy texture of the chocolate box.

Of course, this is not a way to serve food everyday. 'But it is so exciting to think about food more conceptually, to think of it as something more decorative and creative. This is fanciful food, theatrical food, wonderful food, food for the eyes and the spirit as much as for the stomach. It is about taste in every sense of the word.'

What comes out of her decorative pantry is food that is visually exquisite, offset by that snap of spontaneity. For example, tobacco-coloured mocha sticks are wrapped up in a paper napkin from a Milanese café, or else served out of a tiny Henri Bendel shopping bag. 'I have a weakness for the chocolate stripes on those bags,' confesses Quartermaine, as if she were owning up to a weakness for chocolate itself. 'They are just so *My Fair Lady*,' she explains. And with that, the image of Audrey Hepburn as Eliza Doolittle at the races, dressed in a broad-striped Empire-line gown, pops into your mind, and you immediately see her point. And then there is the piece of chocolate-brown silk taffeta (surely something that delicious should not be calorie-free) onto which those mocha

sticks have been crumbled, and somehow the combination of the confection and the silk seems rather dangerous.

It is about the choice of elements — a choice of ornaments that takes the presentation of food into another dimension. And when the ornamentation is as pretty as those paper flutes or as simple as cutting a heart from the pages of the *Financial Times*, the art of food can be transformed into one of the most glamorous, sensual and pleasurable modes of self-expression.

What Quartermaine manages to express in all her decorative ideas is a certain modern glamour, a delicious lightness of touch. She will take two apples and three pears and wrap them in pages pulled from a French chemistry book, in a more sophisticated version of the bright oranges that you see in the market, wrapped in blue tissue paper and packed in rough crates. But when the fruit is placed on a yellow tissue tablecloth, delicately patterned with stars that Cocteau might have scrawled, it looks as beautiful as a seventeenth-century Dutch still-life. The magic is in the mix: the fruit looks at once like a set of

Wintry set pieces of powdery white and glowing caramel — a towering cone of meringues drizzled with spun sugar and an over-the-top twiggy basket filled with ice-cream and set in a drift of icing sugar. This is a composition that appears frozen in time, marking ephemeral moments of pure drama.

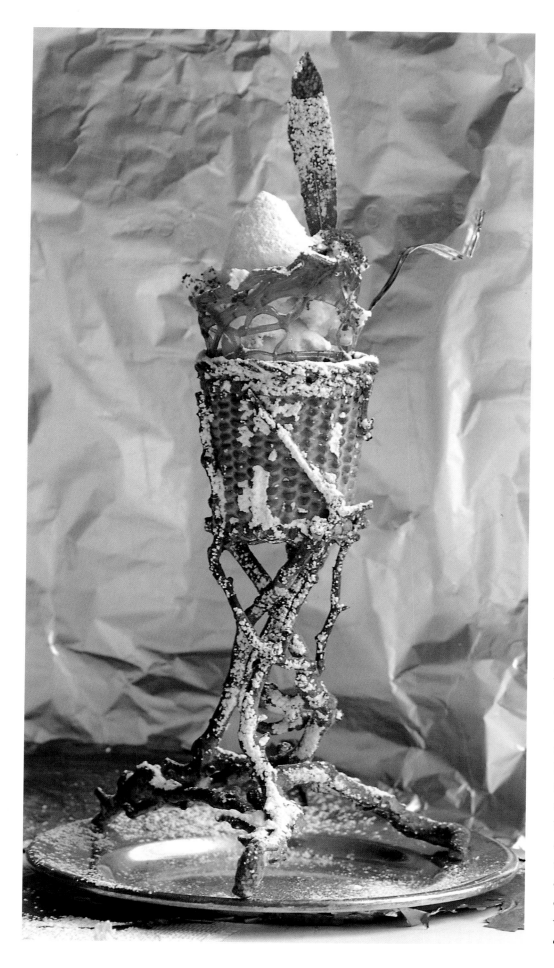

holy relics laid out on an altar, and yet entirely available. After all, what could be more simple than wrapping pears in paper and quickly crayonning some stars onto a sheet of tissue?

It is this looseness, this instant approach, that makes for Quartermaine's particular brand of glamorous informality. Decorative objects, like ornate tea cups and saucers, are used with a lightness of touch. 'I love old china,' says Quartermaine, 'but I am not interested in things that match in sets. I would much rather have a tea tray that had all sorts of different cups on it and eat off plates with different patterns.' So, yes, the china that she buys might be English 1820s; the rim of the plate she picked up for a song in an antique shop might be an eye-popping turquoise blue; or she might be taken by a Regency coffee-can because of its swirly gold pattern. But the effect created when she lays out this eclectic collection of china is neither 'grannyish' nor pompous. She manages, by dint of juxtaposing the formal with the instant, the decorative with the restrained, to create a piquant, bohemian style. Who else would up-end a paint can to retrieve the rubbery sediment, knowing that the bizarre crocodile skin effect would dramatically offset the opalescent gleam of two pears in their spun sugar basket better than any linen tablecloth? In fact, china and linen, unless they come in the purest form possible, have to work quite hard to make it onto Quartermaine's exacting table. Instead, her head is filled with ideas of photocopied tablecloths, or of delicate filo-pastry nests piled high

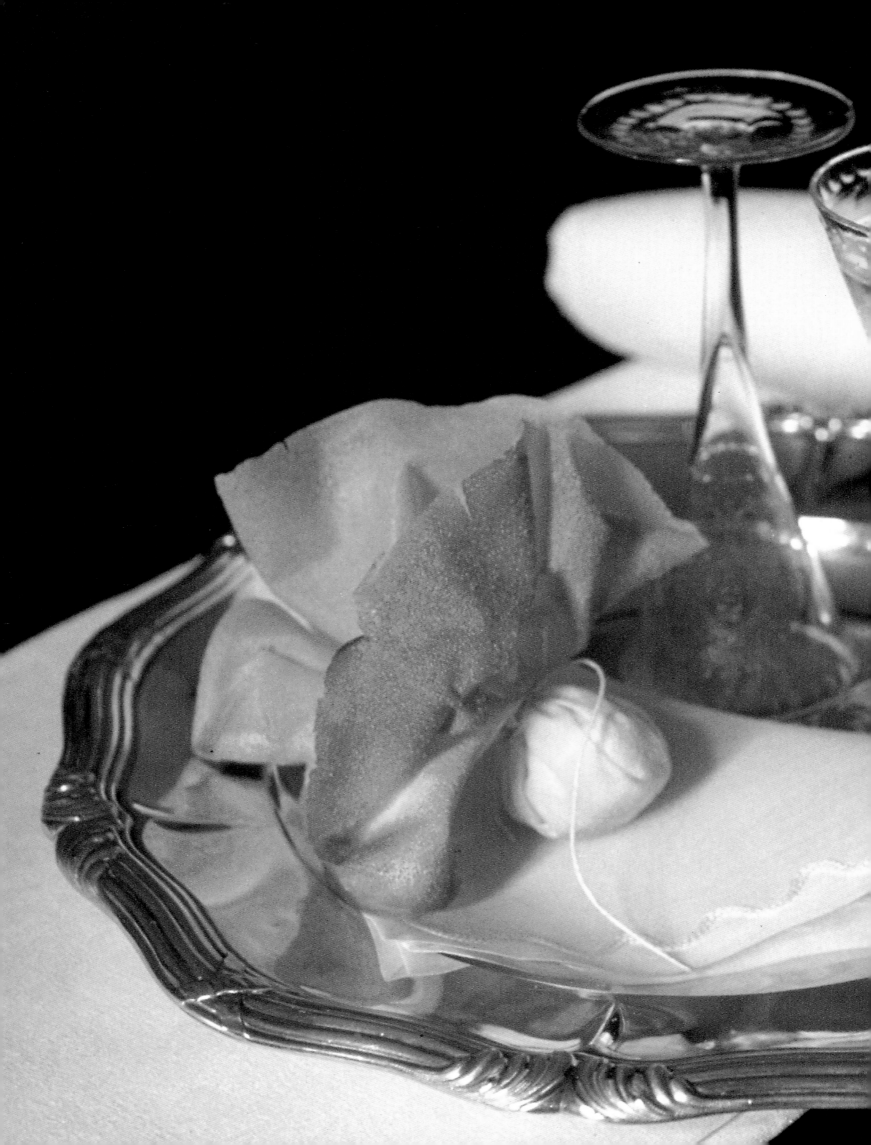

on the open pages of an old book — the flaking leaves of golden pastry matching the yellowing sheaves of paper.

This love of words, of paper and of books seems particularly appropriate when you start to pick on the narrative quality of Quartermaine's food fantasies. It is as if she is telling a story with her creations. A crazy nineteenth-century twiggy basket, found in an antique shop in Norfolk, is transformed into a tiny snow scene when it is filled with brandied cream and coated in icing sugar.

Also fantastical is that towering cone of meringues, with caramel dripping down and the whole confection dredged in icing sugar. It is very fine, very beautiful. 'But what I love about it, is that it is instant,' enthuses Quartermaine. 'It isn't laboured; those meringues were put on really very quickly, there had to be a feeling of things being created in a moment.'

A bay leaf, also dusted with sugar, looks as if it has been covered in frost, and the stiff gold tie that wraps a small

Often, the combination of the simplest elements work best. A silver tray, etched crystal glasses filled with champagne and a starched linen napkin create a moment of pale light and mellow ochre reflections.

Between Quartermaine's edible delicacies and their presentation echoes reverberate as though in a hall of mirrors: the vellum-like edges of old paper are like the layers of filo pastry; spun sugar recalls cross-hatching or spidery italic script; lines scored carelessly on a poached pear echo the printed design on a sheet of cellophane.

cellophane bag of Japanese sweets could be a weathervane. It has something to do with the silver dish and the background of crumpled foil (the plain kitchen variety) — all those silvery, reflective surfaces — that makes this still-life reminiscent of C.S. Lewis's imaginary world of Narnia. 'Or maybe a formal French garden in winter, with clipped topiary and frozen bay trees standing under a light dusting of snow.' She loves scenes such as this for their fragile delicacy — the twigs look as if they could snap at any moment, and the spun-sugar basket is perched precariously like a miniature tree house. Basic ingredients, like sugar, silver foil or a scoop of cream, are turned into pure fantasy.

Another element of her taste in food is her abiding passion for colour. So assured is her palette that she uses the ingredients

as paints to make a picture. She finds the garish colours of a scoop of candy as appealing as a row of nail-varnish bottles. 'I love the psychedelic colours you get in cheap sweets,' she admits. 'They are quite the brightest pinks, the brightest greens.' It can be no mistake that they seem to duplicate the tangle of silks that spill onto the floor from her worktable. The delicate yellow of the tiny mimosa sweets are nothing unless they can be filtered through the soft lilac of a Venetian glass. What stands in for the lace tablecloth? What else but the cheapest mesh bag from a local fruit shop.

She has an extraordinary ability to present food in a totally unexpected way. Partly, it stems from her ability to substitute whimsical details — a furl of white paper napkin stands in for a swirl of cream, turning a dessert into a sculptural form in the process — and partly it comes from her love of wrapping and exquisite packaging. Cellophane is an instant glamorizer. Wrapped elaborately around boxes containing small biscuits, or twisted into bags for Japanese sweets and tied with a ribbon, it has the effect of making food somehow untouchable, and therefore more tempting and desirable. But in Quartermaine's hands, of course, it is scarcely unpacked before she has handprinted it with curlicues, turning it into tablecloths that look like they have been made from frozen water, those gilded words and scrolls trapped inside the ice. And if food can be set on the open pages of a book, why not turn delicate *tuiles amandes* into a unique edible version of those pages by scrawling each one in curly script? Not only is it pretty, but it is witty — there can surely be no more appealing way to, literally, eat your words.

And if the food can be wrapped or treated like a present, so too can the table furniture. It is all part of Quartermaine's ability to set the scene, to tell a story. So metal chairs might be given organza skirts, which make them look for all the world like ballerinas. Their fluted skirts might then be picked up in the shape of a brandy-snap basket piled high with raspberries. It is all about bringing a personal touch to the feast. Wine in this instance is a bottle with a beautiful handwritten label from La Colombe D'Or, the legendary hotel and restaurant in the south of France, favoured by the likes of Picasso. 'I love

it there,' says Quartermaine. 'You can eat outside in a lovely garden surrounded by sculpture. You choose your food from these huge sheets of watercolour paper onto which the day's menu has been beautifully painted.' Everywhere there are simple flowers arranged loosely in little vases, 'And by the pool, near the Calder mobile, there is a sculpture of a giant green apple by Hans Hedberg. It's one of those places where art and food are integrated harmoniously, and with consideration to the aesthetic of the whole experience.'

Of course, food has this ability to transport, and in creating these tableaux Quartermaine can be transported to wherever she wants to go. The ballerina chairs came from a memory of a cake shop in Aix-en-Provence. 'I remember walking into a *pâtisserie* and it was just like a drawing come to life, like an illustration in a book from my childhood,' she explains. 'In the centre, there was an enormous cake stand, tiers and tiers of which were piled high with cakes and sweets and other confectionary. And on shelves in front of mirrors, there was the very French idea of having boxes and boxes of jellies and candied fruits on their sides. The whole arrangement was stunning.'

Of course, Quartermaine will be able to satisfy anyone's appetite for beauty, but perfection she finds a little less palatable. 'A perfectly laid table can be a little daunting for me,' she admits. 'But the moment the table begins to be used, the glasses filled, the plates moved, the napkins thrown down, that's when things start to get really interesting.'

Packaging and wrapping are a passion. Cellophane wrapping, a fine paper box and an organza shift falling off a chair create a setting of exquisite fragility and delicacy for dainty Japanese sweets. The sweets themselves are stamped with tiny flowers in muted pastel shades, or glow with the luminous colours of intermingled glass beads. See-through openwork chairs are dressed in frothy layers of filmy transparency and conjure up irresistible images of ballerinas in the wings and tinkling conversations in a French salon de thé.

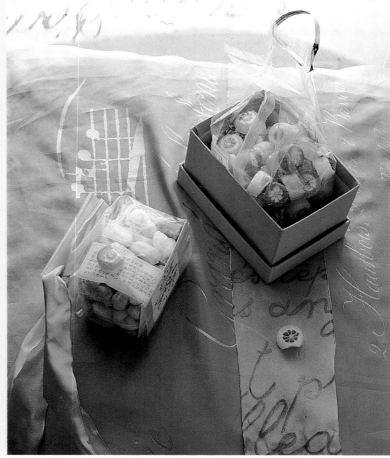

Flowers

'I WENT TO A ROSE FARM JUST OUTSIDE MARRAKESH TO BUY FLOWERS FOR A VIDEO THAT WAS BEING FILMED IN MOROCCO. EVERYWHERE YOU LOOKED THERE WERE ACRES OF ROSES AND EVERY DAY THE FLOWERS WERE FRESHLY PICKED. THE HEADS WERE VERY SMALL, VERY COMPACT, DOTS OF PURE COLOUR, AND WE STOOD AND CHOSE THE COLOURS WE WANTED. YOU COULD HAVE ANYTHING: SCARLET, FUCHSIA, YELLOW, ORANGE. I PAID FOR THE ROSES AND LOADED THE BOXES INTO THE CAR.

'SETTING UP THE VIDEO TOOK HOURS. IT WAS HOT. THE DIRECTOR WANTED A FOUNTAIN FILLED. WHEN THAT WAS DONE, I TOOK THE BOXES OF ROSES AND EMPTIED THEM ONTO THE WATER. AND THEN, AS IT WAS SO HOT AND THE PETALS LOOKED SO BEAUTIFUL FLOATING ON THE SURFACE, I THREW MYSELF IN TOO. THERE IS SOMETHING SO ROMANTIC ABOUT HAVING YOUR WHOLE BODY IMMERSED IN WATER THAT HAS BEEN TURNED INTO A SEA OF PETALS. YOU LOOKED DOWN AND ALL YOU SAW WERE LIQUID FLOWERS. THAT MOMENT SUMS UP EVERYTHING THAT I LOVE ABOUT FLOWERS.'

Seeing through to their essence — clear colour, soft sculpture, pure perfume — Quartermaine layers and arranges fresh flowers like papers for a collage.

'I love flowers when they are just on the point of turning. . . . Rusting petals that look as if they have been brushed with watercolour.'

In the way she decorates with flowers, as in everything else she does, Quartermaine's trick is to appear spontaneous. Flowers are loosely scattered rather than formally arranged, laid on beautiful plates rather than forced into bowls, pinned to a drape of white cotton which is then hung on a wall rather than always being left at table height. When they are treated this way, flowers become romantic, surreal objects in an artistic landscape. And there is scarcely a vase in sight.

It is a look that succeeds because she seems to have peered into the heart of each flower and seen it as colour, scent and soft sculptural form. In a sense, it is her artist's eye working overtime, disregarding formalities and creating surprising new takes on what flowers can bring to a room. And when she looks at them like this, amazing things start to happen.

In a way she uses flowers to suggest, well, flowers. And as a result, none of their spontaneity, their freshness, their blowzy abandon is lost when she snips them from their stems and carries them from the garden into a room. In fact, the words 'cultivation', 'arrangement', and 'formality' have no space in her floral lexicon. Overbearing, stiff arrangements are happily ditched in favour of a looser, more spontaneous approach. 'I don't like formal arrangements,' she says. 'I like flowers to be mixed together, tumbling and falling.' And so it is that with this intensely artistic approach, the flowers are used as drops of colour, like pools of pigment on a canvas.

When flowers get this painterly, it can scarcely come as any surprise that the waxy perfection of an orchid is not something

A looser approach to flower arranging. When formality is provided by the room, armfuls of blooms — buddleia, roses and delphiniums — may be strewn with apparent abandon and still look composed, like a flower-print textile design from the 1920s. Even an element as unobtrusive as the grid pattern, ironed into the cloth, helps to lend a sense of structure to their evanescence.

she would prize, preferring instead the largesse of peonies, with their soft colours and their heads heavy as if they were drunk on rainwater. And she adores old-fashioned cottage roses, the mosses and the gallicas, with their mass of crinkled petals as full-blown as a silk rosette. 'There is a moment when roses are at their most beautiful,' she notes, 'and that is just when they are beginning to turn. If it's possible, they are even more lovely when they are dying.'

Once the flowers are cut, she starts to mix, layering colours and shapes much as she would the papers for one of her collages. Roses bed down comfortably with field flowers or stately stems straight from an English cutting garden. Canterbury bells, foxgloves, campanula or cornflowers are all favourites.

One of the conventions of English country-house style is the liberal use of chintz, as rambling roses trounce across length after length of printed delphiniums and hyacinths. When Quartermaine snipped the head off a buddleia and placed it on a starched white tablecloth, she was translating those rather classical elements into something a little more modern. This, then, is chintz for the modern era, the floral shapes literally blossoming out of two dimensions and into three.

If nothing is lost by bringing the garden, in its freshest form, inside, then Quartermaine is also happy to take elements of her apartment out into the garden in an elegant cross-fertilization of interior design and horticulture. She brings nature in by growing pots of lavender or standard myrtles, climbing roses and even clematis, on the balcony and then whisking them

through her French windows where they turn her sitting room into a beautifully furnished topiary garden. She also manages to persuade cornflowers, foxgloves and other field flowers to grow out of old terracotta pots (yes, it really does work) and then places them next to her gilded furniture for a hint of Marie-Antoinette rusticity. In a witty reversal of this indoor-outdoor theme, tulips on the artist's balcony look wonderful when they sprout up out of pretty old china bowls. In fact, she decorates her balcony much as she does her interiors. Rusting French metal chairs go inside or outside depending on whim and weather. On tables, huge chunks of architectural plasterwork have been piled up amongst a collection of stones and shells. Daisy trees are grown in large flower pots to add height, while the leaves of a small lavender bush, looking for all the world as if they have been lightly dusted with silver, protrude from a large conch shell.

Often she will even keep a bunch of irises on the table just outside the window, as if the balcony were no more than another room to step into. (This is especially appealing in the winter when the cold weather helps to keep the flowers fresh.) There might even be a lemon tree for a spot of nursery-rhyme nostalgia and in her own version of *The Singing Ringing Tree*, she might then hang silver apples, golden pears, and a crystal chandelier drop or two from its branches.

Inside, she might grow a garden — or at least appear to. When art directing a pop-music video, Quartermaine first whitewashed the floor and then pushed cut flowers

in between the cracks in the floorboards. 'The effect was very surreal, very magical, and also very beautiful,' she recalls. But with flowers she decorates with more than colour and shape; there is scent, too. And it has a powerful effect on the senses. 'Scent is very important. So buying flowers at different times of the year can be exhilarating.' Her favourite bouquet? 'Roses are the best perfume,' she says simply. 'They don't take over a room, they layer it with their scent.'

For Quartermaine, flowers are just one more element of surprise and romance. For her, they become living props, adding colour and shape, intensifying a mood, heightening the drama. When she piled them up onto a cake stand, they could almost have been a mouthwatering selection from a Viennese pastry shop, the petals made from icing sugar or marzipan. 'What I really loved was the way the whole composition — the stand, the roses — became so sculptural,' she explains. And despite the fact that these hybrid tea roses were a riot of colour, from blush pink to lemon yellow, the entire scene was still very simple. The flowers were allowed to float in plenty of white space, their extraordinary colours enhanced by the bareness of the wall behind.

And if roses can be placed decoratively on a cake stand, they can also become a corsage, pinned to a dress where the warmth of a woman's décolletage will release the scent. Why not pretend that a chair is an evening dress, similarly in need of adornment? Pinned to a knot of lime-green fabric which has been tied around a chair, a rose becomes part of a

Flowers are the most exquisite accessories for any room. Quartermaine presents a delicately poised marriage of formality and looseness, balancing colour — from burnt orange, fiery crimsons and reds to the palest pink — and contrast, in a selection of flowers served up on a tall wirework cake stand. Hoodwinking the senses, a languorous shell-pink cabbage rose, loosely tied into a knot of apple-green cotton, seems to fill the air with perfume even from the printed page. Quartermaine's love affair with flowers is captured in this eulogy to the amaryllis.

Amaryllis!
Volubilis!
Lisse est le lis
Dont la prière
Est de senteur!
J'en ai pris hier
Pour plus de cent heures.

wonderfully loose interpretation of where flowers should be situated and what they add to a composition.

It might seem a leap, but not for someone whose work has such an affinity with fashion and costume. Her current inspiration is Madeleine Vionnet, the genius couturière of the 1920s and 1930s who had an absolute obsession with roses. She loved to have them printed onto fabric that looked like lengths of sheer silver tissue. Then, in a feat of technical virtuosity, she would take a single piece of this fabric and work with it until she had a perfect bias-cut, petal-pleat dress. It was because of this artistry, rigour and inventiveness that her work has been lionized by the fashion cognoscenti and indeed anyone who is interested in where fashion stops and art begins.

'I have a deep admiration for Vionnet,' admits Quartermaine. 'I had just done the picture with the organza and roses when I saw a book on her work. I opened the pages at random, and there was a photograph of this sheer silver organza dress over-printed with roses . . . I felt positively overwhelmed.'

Flowers are the mood makers. Rose petals laid in a trail or scattered on bare floorboards, delphiniums and peonies tied into loose bundles and then laid on a chair seat, can look more romantic than any floral carpet or piece of chintz. There is something about their colour, their scent and their sheer fragility that gives the rooms they are in an air of expectancy. Needing flowers to dress the formal interior of a French château, Quartermaine simply went out into the

These and previous pages: Quartermaine prizes the informality of garden flowers in a formal setting. Cow parsley and cranesbill make an exquisite set dressing. The inky blue spires of larkspurs hang about an open doorway, whilst the chalky grey of the paintwork and chairs provide a muted backdrop to the flowers.

gardens and fields around the house in the early morning and gathered armfuls of whatever she could find. Rather than forcing her floral finds into bunches and then the bunches into vases, it seemed more natural, and more beautiful, just to tie them loosely and hang them around a door handle or pin the end of a ribbon to the ceiling and let the flowers spill down.

There is something cinematic about this looser and more romantic approach to arranging flowers. Looking into those rooms, after she had dressed them, was rather like watching a scene from a Visconti movie before the actors arrived on set. 'As we put the flowers around,' remembers Quartermaine, 'the afternoon heat started to press in, and with the light just breaking in through the half-closed shutters, it was as if we were in Sicily and this was siesta time. . . .'

And for the close-ups in this mood movie, there were soft-focus, impressionistic sketches of roses drawn on salon chairs upholstered in ivory silk and a fine blue-and-white stripe. The delicacy of a fresh flower was preserved in the brush strokes which had been painted quickly, keeping everything light — with just enough of the blue rose to suggest its heavier-petalled, living counterpart. The muted palette of pale blues, greys and whites has an air of serenity about it, as if this were a film shot in the half-tones somewhere between colour and black-and-white. 'There are moments that are very special,' says Quartermaine, 'and there was something about those chairs that made them look as if they had a personality of their own, as if they were arriving at a party.'

Flowers, fabrics and paper shift and echo across visual boundaries, sharpening our perceptions in an exhilarating intensity of texture and colour.

Many artists seem to have this extra-ordinary affinity with flowers. She cites Klimt and his mesmerizing flower paintings, the rich autumnal colours set off by the pristine white of a fence, or Bonnard and his droplets of colour. Quartermaine, too, shares this fascination, but she does not stop at painting flowers; she plays with them, placing a real iris over a flower painted onto a plate. It could be the real-life version of what is underneath, or maybe she thinks that it looks good enough to eat. 'I love the idea of flowers where you least expect them,' she says. 'Often for parties I have hung long-stemmed flowers like gladioli from chandeliers so that your eye is drawn up to this burst of fiery orange.' Or she has woven branches of apple blossoms through stair balustrades, or used them to garland a mantelpiece.

Again, this playing with elements is about witty reversals; a quiet jab at sleepy preconceptions. Flowers can be laid on chairs as if the fabric has sprung to life, or lightly sketched onto ivory silk as if they have been pressed onto the pages of a book. And in a sense, by hanging her flowers from ribbons, she is merely giving them back their stalks, albeit reversing the direction they grow in the process.

'Flowers have to transport you,' she maintains. 'They have to take you to places of intrigue and romance.'

It is a feeling that, for her, is summed up by the garden of sculptor and jeweller, Claude Lalanne and her husband and fellow sculptor, François-Xavier. The land around their converted dairy farm in France is an enchanted place, where enormous bronze birds perch underneath trees, metal sheep look as if they are grazing

A real iris surmounts the painted flower, its velvety depth of colour enhanced by the proximity of its porcelain image; while garden flowers are chosen with care to make a flower chandelier.
Previous page: Roses laid on a turquoise chair reminded Quartermaine of Istanbul. In this way, flowers can conjure up lived experiences. Overleaf: The magical dream garden of the senses.

'*Apart from spending time in my studio, being in an overgrown garden is the next best thing.*'

on the long, sweet grass and alliums appear to move in stately progression across the confines of a walled kitchen garden, stepping carefully between cabbages which have been allowed to run to seed. Behind the shocking pink of a rambling rose, which has been grown up through the acid green of an apple tree, stands what else but a large, blue, metal hippopotamus.

'I always loved *The Secret Garden*, by Frances Hodgson Burnett, when I was a child,' says Quartermaine in explanation of why she is so drawn to this alchemical garden where elements are changed, rearranged, and then transformed into something else. 'There is a feeling that the statues are only sleeping and can come to life.' Walled gardens, or potagers, like the one at the Lalanne's house in Fontainebleau, just seem to intensify the mystery. 'There is a mysterious air of secrecy about that garden; you could believe it holds all sorts of magical properties, that there is treasure buried in every corner and that the statues could move towards you at any moment.'

And, of course, Quartermaine has an instinctive feeling for space and placement, for plants as living paint on an ever-growing canvas, rather than simply as ways to fill a border. Claude Lalanne presses flower shapes into service in her jewels and her sculpture; similarly, Quartermaine uses them on her furniture and in her interiors. There is an aesthetic at work which pushes boundaries, liberating the workaday; the everyday into a fairy-tale dimension.

Magic, romance, alchemy, call it what you will. It is only art by another name.

Sources

Carolyn Quartermaine fabric collections are available through the following retailers and distributers. Those also supplying her furniture and accessories are denoted by an asterisk (*). For any further details please contact:

Carolyn Quartermaine
P.O.Box 12870
London SW5 9WG

UNITED KINGDOM
* Maryse Boxer & Carolyn Quartermaine @ Joseph Maison
26 Sloane Street
London SW1X 7LQ
Tel/Fax: (0)171 245 9493

FRANCE
* Gladys Mougin
30 Rue de Lille
Paris 75007
Tel: 33 (0)1 40 20 0833
Fax: 33 (0)1 40 20 0922

GERMANY
Charles Koenig Associates
Hornbeam
Dorney Wood Road
Burnham, Bucks SLI 8EH
England
Tel: (0)1628 662700
Fax: (0)1628 667728

AUSTRIA
Mandy Neumann
'La Puce'
Rainerstrasse 10
4020 Linz
Tel: 43 (0)732 658168

SPAIN
Camilla Hamm
Aspectos
C/REC 28
Barcelona

Tel: 34 (0)3 319 5285
Fax: 34 (0)3 268 4983

ITALY
* Teresa Ginori
Eclectica
Corso Garibaldi 3
Milan 20121
Tel: 39 (0)287 6194
Fax: 39 (0)287 7810

PORTUGAL
Viterbo
Travessa de Santa Catarina
Patio do Lancastre 15
1200 Lisboa
Tel: 351 (0)1 346 2479
Fax: 351 (0)1 346 3494

HOLLAND
* Karin Blom
Middelie 76
1472 GS Middelie
Tel: 31 (0)299 621 242
Fax: 31 (0)299 623 296

SCANDINAVIA
* Eric Moyland Andersen
Interior Plus
Grevturegatan 57
S–11438
Stockholm
Sweden
Tel: 46 (0)8 665 3118
Fax: 46 (0)8 665 3119
(Distribution includes Sweden, Norway, Denmark, Finland and Iceland)

* Lau Aabling
EGE Art Line
20th Century Masters
    Collection
EGE Axminster A/S
230 Grejsdalsvej
7100 Vejle
Denmark
Tel: 45 75 83 3300
Fax: 45 75 72 0696

(International distribution, rug collection)

SWITZERLAND
Christa Burton
Burton Interiors
Rosengarten Weg 1
Obberieden CH8942
Tel: 41 (0)1 720 7320
Fax: 41 (0)1 720 2450

USA
Christopher Hyland Inc.
D&D Building
979 Third Avenue
Suite 1710
New York
NY 10022
Tel: 1 (0)212 688 6121
Fax: 1 (0)212 688 6176

Agnes Bourne Inc.
2 Henry Adams Street
Showroom 220
San Francisco
CA 94103
Tel: 1 (0)415 626 6883
Fax: 1 (0)415 626 2489

* Linda Chase Associates Inc.
482 Town Street
East Haddam
CT 06423
Tel: 1 (0)860 873 9499
Fax: 1 (0)860 873 9796

* Amanda Halstead Designs
525 East 72nd Street 33 # C
New York
NY 10021
Tel: 1 (0)212 879 1090
Fax: 1 (0)212 879 1090

* Interior Planning Consultants
P.O. Box 3207
Meridian
MS 39305
Tel: 1 (0)601 693 1668
Fax: 1 (0)601 485 8301

* Waldo Fernandez
620 North Almont Drive
Los Angeles
CA 90069
Tel: 1 (0)310 278 1803
Fax: 1 (0)310 278 4596

CANADA
Primavera
160 Pears Avenue
Suite 210
Toronto, M5R 1T2
Tel: 1 (0)416 921 3334
Fax: 1 (0)416 921 3227

AUSTRALIA
Robin Valkenburg
Cambric
485 Glenferrie Road
Kooyong
Victoria 3144
Tel: 61 (0)3 804 3804
Fax: 61 (0)3 804 3485

NEW ZEALAND
Christopher Gee
Rileys Ltd.
2B Garfield Street
Parnell
Auckland
Tel: 64 (0)9 309 7646
Fax: 64 (0)9 309 4582

Mailing address:
P.O.Box 91509
A.M.SC.
New Zealand

SOUTH AFRICA
Marguerite MacDonald
Mavromac Ltd.
P.O.Box 76178
Wendywood 2144
Tel: 27 (0)11 444 1584
Fax: 27 (0)11 444 1541
Tel: 27 (0)21 797 4739
    (Cape Town office)
Tel 27 (0)31 29 3609
    (Durban office)

Index

Acknowledgments

AUTHOR'S ACKNOWLEDGMENTS

I wish to extend my warmest thanks to everyone who helped out on this book, especially Christopher Griffin, Bruce Poole and Olivier Couillaud of Chez Bruce, Caroline Lebeau, Jean Louis Mennesson of Chateau d'Outrelaisse, Zanna (The Ragged School), Annabel Lewis at V.V. Rouleux, Sahco Hesslein, Bodil Tamnhed (who allowed me to keep her funiture for ages), Carolyn Daly, Ruth Forman, Petra Kormann, Claude and François Xavier Lalanne for their magical garden, Anna Thomas, Wild at Heart and Gilding the Lily (flowers), Thrifty Van Rental, Paul Franzosi at Set Pieces, Malabar, Sharyn Storrier-Lyneham, Fix-a-Frame, Pete Smith, John Wright, Nigel Stone, Charles Rutherfoord, Lelievre, Isabelle Corbani, Julie Contreras, Margaret Bradham, Bob Warrens and Bob and Maryse Boxer.

Special thanks go to Jacques Dirand, without whose wonderful eye and expertise this book would not have been the same.

Finally, I wish to thank Kate Constable who worked tirelessly on the text with me and the wonderful team at Conran Octopus: Helen Lewis, Catriona Woodburn and Denny Hemming who allowed me such creative freedom on this book.

PUBLISHER'S ACKNOWLEDGMENTS

Conran Octopus would like to thank the following photographers and organizations for their permission to reproduce the photographs in this book:

10 Steve Dalton/Vogue Entertaining; 12-13 Ingalill Snitt/World of Interiors/Condé Nast Publications; 17 Brigitte Lacombe; 18-19 **below** Noelle Höeppe; 24 Jacques Dirand; 26 Christine Osbourne Pictures; 28 Jean Pierre Godeaut; 33 Jean Pierre Godeaut; 35 **below** J-N Reichel/Agence Top; 42 Roland Beaufre/Agence Top; 43 **below** Carlos Navajas/The Image Bank; 54 Roland Beaufre/Agence Top; 55 Darderian/Wallis; 60 **right** Jean Pierre Godeaut; 61 **right** Pratt-Pries/Diaf; 68 **above, left** © Union Francaise des Arts du Costume; 68 **above, right** Pascal Chevallier/Agence Top; 68 **below** © Union Francaise des Arts du Costume; 72 © Union Francaise des Arts du Costume; 80 From *Fabrics* by Caroline Lebeau. © 1984 by Caroline Lebeau and Jaque Dirand. Reprinted by permission of Clarkson N. Potter, a division of Crown Publishers, Inc.; 90 **above, right & below** Pascal Chevallier/Agence Top; 91 Steve Dalton/Vogue Entertaining; 102 Ingalill Snitt/World of Interiors/Condé Nast; 103 San Francisco Museum of Modern Art. Acquired through a gift of Peggy Guggenheim/ © ARS, NY and DACS, London 1997; 106 Ann Rogers/Refocus; 107 Eric Morin; 111 **centre** J. Lautier/Image du Sud; 117 Fundacio Joan Miro/© ADAGP, Paris & DACS, London 1997; 123 Steve Dalton/Vogue Entertaining; 130 Edward Boubat/Agence Top; 132-133 Pascal Chevallier/Agence Top; 139 Steve Dalton/Vogue Entertaining; 140 Simon Brown/Elle Decoration; 143 **above** Pascal Chevallier/Agence Top; 148 Jane Gifford; 154-155 Alexandre Bailhache (Garden of François & Claude Lalanne).

Every effort has been made to trace the copyright holders, artists and designers. We apologies in advance for any unintentional omission and would be pleased to insert the appropriate acknowledgment in subsequent editions.

Additional thanks to Barbara Mellor, Maria Leach, Helen Wire, Christa Weil, Katherine Adzima, and Gillian Delaforce.